Horseshoe –
S.J.CA.

Healing Through the Mass

Healing Through the Mass

Robert DeGrandis, S.S.J.
with Linda Schubert

Revised Edition

Resurrection Press
An Imprint of
CATHOLIC BOOK PUBLISHING CORP.
Totowa • New Jersey

Imprimatur: Most Reverend James Chan
 Bishop of Melaka - Johor, Malaysia
 February 21, 1992

Revised edition published in 1992 by

 Catholic Book Publishing/Resurrection Press
 77 West End Road
 Totowa, NJ 07512
 www.catholicbookpublishing.com

ISBN 13: 978-1-878718-10-5

Library of Congress Catalog Card Number: 91-68523

Cover design: John Murello

Printed in the United States of America.

Contents

PART V
CONCLUDING RITE

Acknowledgements

A special "thank you" is extended to all who contributed to this book. I am grateful to my former editor, Jessie Borrello of New Orleans, Louisiana, for her assistance on the first edition of *Healing through the Mass.* Her significant contributions helped to lay the foundations for this current edition. Appreciation is extended to Ken and Charlene Lawson of Gretna, Louisiana for their valuable contributions to the first edition. Rose Payne of New Orleans, Louisiana, Mary Lozano of Fresno, California, Jennifer Hieronymous of Mobile, Alabama, and Sister Barbara Vaughn, O.S.B. of Birmingham, Alabama, also made important contributions to the first edition. My gratitude is extended to each of them. A special thanks to my sister, Dorothea DeGrandis Sudol, and my friends, too numerous to mention, who inspired me with their living of the Holy Mass day by day.

A note of thanks to Sister Rosemary Ford, O.S.B., of Yankton, South Dakota, and Father Ralph Weishaar, O.F.M., of San Diego, California, for reading an early draft of the revised edition and adding valuable comments. Appreciation is extended to the people who responded to the *Healing through the Mass* survey in the current edition. Their heartfelt responses and valuable insights are greatly appreciated. Finally, I owe a special debt of gratitude to my brother priests for their example of faithful service in the holy sacrifice of the Mass.

Preface

During the meal Jesus took bread, blessed it, broke it, and gave it to His disciples. 'Take this and eat it,' He said, 'this is my body.' Then He took a cup, gave thanks, and gave it to them. 'All of you must drink from it,' He said, 'for this is my blood, the blood of the covenant, to be poured out in behalf of many for the forgiveness of sins. (Mt 26:26-28).

Marsha was a Jewish actress married to a disk jockey in London. One night when she was distraught about some problems a woman appeared to her in a vision and told her to go and find a church. She went out into the night and wandered around, eventually finding herself standing in front of the rectory of a Catholic church. When the pastor opened the door she said simply, "I'm here for the bread of life." The priest was captivated by her story, and began to talk to her about the Catholic faith.

When Marsha was eventually baptized she described it as a cleansing rain soaking through her whole being. When she received the Eucharist she said it was like being totally consumed by the love of Christ. Her amazing conversion had a powerful effect on many people.

The sacrifice of the Mass is the very heart of our faith and central to our relationship with God. In the Mass the great mystery of the life, death and resurrection of the Lord Jesus Christ is celebrated in a sacramental way so that we might partake of that life. As we enter in, receive, and apply the benefits of this all-consuming act of love we are changed, converted and healed. A primary purpose of this book is to help Catholics to do just that. It is written for all Catholics-priests, religious and laity. It is also for those who may be observing the Church from a distance for various reasons.

Throughout the book I will discuss the essential parts of the Mass and emphasize the healing dimensions. In this newly revised and expanded edition we have included results from 100 respondents to a survey on *Healing through the Mass*. The purpose of the survey was to gain "bits of wisdom" on healing elements in Mass from people around the country, and find out what they would like amplified in the current edition. They requested amplification on many areas in the book. They want to know about mercy, covenant, the sign of peace, and want a deeper look at *The Lord's Prayer*. They have asked for more testimonies from people who have been healed through the Mass. There was a sense of frustration in some respondents—an awareness that healing ought to be a natural outflow of the Mass, but somehow it was eluding them. They want to know why, and what to do about it.

We also received several responses to a priests' survey that included the same basic questions with one exception. We asked the priests, "What can we, as priests, do to open people to the Mass?" Responses to all the questionnaires are summarized in the Appendix as well as referenced in various places throughout the book.

The traditional Catholic teachings on the Eucharistic celebration as a banquet of the Lord and also as a sacrifice are familiar to many. As the Second Vatican Council states: "At the Last Supper, on the night He was betrayed, our Savior instituted the Eucharistic Sacrifice of His Body and Blood. This He did in order to perpetuate the sacrifice of the Cross throughout the ages until He should come again, and so to entrust to His beloved Spouse, the Church, a memorial of His death and resurrection: a sacrament of love, a sign of unity, a bond of charity, a paschal banquet in which Christ is consumed, the mind is filled with grace, and a pledge of future glory is given to us." [1]

In recent years there has been renewed focus on the Mass as a healing service. Ted Dobson speaks of the heritage of healing through the Eucharist in *Say but the Word:* "But in the earliest Christian days, the Eucharist was seen as a sacrament of healing and transformation, a rite that brought wholeness to the people who celebrated it. For example, St. Augustine in his greatest book, *The City of God,* as well as in his last book, *Revisions,* witnessed to the healing he had seen in his own church as a result of people receiving Eucharist." [2] Barbara Shlemon, R.N., in a booklet, *The Healing Power of the Eucharist,* states: "Each time we attend the celebration of Mass, we are at a healing service. As we approach the altar, we pray, 'Lord, I am not worthy to receive You, but only say the word and I shall be healed.' This is a prayer of confidence in the power of Jesus Christ to transform our physical, emotional and spiritual needs. If we truly believe that Jesus is present in the consecrated bread, then we should expect to obtain wholeness as we accept His body into ourselves." [3]

Since 1986 I have conducted seminars for priests in various parts of the United States as well as in the Philippines, Australia, Malaysia, India, Indonesia, Spain, Central and South America. In these "Healing Power of Holy Orders" retreats, I emphasize aspects of the Mass that offer healing. As the priest becomes aware of the healing potential in the Mass, he communicates that increased faith and knowledge to the congregation, and healing begins to be manifested in a greater degree.

I pray for my brother priests that they will receive increased faith in the healing power of the Mass. I pray for everyone who reads this book, that each will become, like Marsha, totally consumed by the love of Christ. I pray, too, for those who have no knowledge of the Lord Jesus Christ, and no understanding of what it means to receive the Bread of Life. Lord, bring them to Your banqueting table, for Your banner over them is love. (Sng 2:4).

This work is dedicated to St. Margaret Clitherow

who was martyred in York, England in 1586. As a non-Catholic, she let her home be used for the celebration of the Eucharist. Seeing the faith and devotion of the persecuted Catholics, she embraced the faith. At 30 years of age she was sentenced to be crushed to death for harboring priests and having Mass in her home. When apprehended, she chose not to deny her faith but embraced the martyrdom of leaving a loving husband and three small children. May we have the faith of those who died for the Mass!

Foreword

It pleases me that Father Robert DeGrandis has titled his new book, *Healing Through the Mass*. For many years I have been convinced that far too little emphasis has been given to the marvelous healing power of our Lord Jesus through the holy sacrifice of the Mass. In recent years many other communities of faith have offered healing services. There is obviously a "hunger" for such. How blessed we Catholics are to have the "ultimate" healing service each day in the Holy Mass. From the beginning to the end of the Mass the healing love and power of the Lord Jesus is manifested. The signs and symbols used at Mass are expressions of the Lord's love and healing — the holy water, the crucifix, and sign of the cross, to mention a few. The penitential rite is a marvelous sign of the Lord's spiritual healing and forgiveness. Through the songs of praise such as the "Gloria" and the "Holy Holy" we encounter the loving, healing mercy of the Lord.

Above all, of course, the Scripture readings make present the love and healing presence of the Lord Jesus. Countless people have testified how the Lord touched them deeply through the proclamation of the inspired Word. This should not be a surprise if we really believe the words of the author of Hebrews: "The Word of God is living and active, sharper than any two-edged sword" (Heb 4:12). Along with His Holy Word, we also are richly graced with the precious Body and Blood of Jesus in the Holy Eucharist. It is significant that you and I pray at each Mass just before Communion, "Lord, I am not worthy to receive You, but only say the word and I shall be healed." Time and time again people have testified to powerful healing — body, mind and spirit — that they have experienced through the most Holy Eucharist. A growing number of Christians of other faiths have developed a deep desire for our Eucharist; for they yearn for the grace, nourishment and healing that flows from the altar.

Thanks be to our loving God who is so bountiful in sharing the healing love and power of His Son Jesus. May we members of His Body open our lives more fully to this bountiful gift, especially as we participate in Holy Mass. I have every confidence that this fine book, *Healing Through The Mass*, will be of great help to you and your loved ones. It is a book that should not be read in just one sitting but rather be an ongoing source of meditation in preparation for Holy Mass.

Paul V. Dudley
Bishop of Sioux Falls

PART I

INTRODUCTION

Healing Places

Anthropologists tell us that men of all faiths, all religions, have always had a sacred place. The earliest holy places were piles of stones, erected as memorials in places where God met man.

The later sacrificial altars were built of earth or stone. In the Greek, the word "altar" means "place of sacrifice."

In the Old Testament we see God calling His people to a sacred place. "When all the work undertaken by Solomon for the temple of the Lord had been completed, he brought in the dedicated offerings of his father David, putting the silver, the gold and all the other articles in the treasuries of the house of God" (2Chr 5:1). The priests consecrated themselves and stood near the altar with cymbals, harps, trumpets and other instruments. Singers praised the Lord, singing: "Give thanks to the Lord for he is good, for his mercy endures forever." The priests were not able to continue, because "...the Lord's glory filled the house of God" (v.14). They were overwhelmed by the power of the Lord.

The Lord is present with His people today in sacred places. Our churches are sacred because of the healing presence of Jesus. In ancient days the glory descended on the temple that contained only symbols of the Lord's presence. How much more should we experience the healing presence of the Lord with the Eucharistic presence of God in our own churches.

From time to time many of us experience anxiety and agitation before walking into a church, we sense the presence of the Lord, and all the tension and anxiety disappear. I have had that same experience many times, especially in the Church of the Immaculate Conception, the Jesuit Church on Baronne Street in New Orleans, Louisiana. Sometimes I visit that church on a hot summer day. The coolness and quietness of the church speak powerfully of the Lord's waiting presence. His presence is felt in that church because it is a long-time gathering place for people of prayer.

As you enter a Catholic church, consider the healing elements in the environment. The crucifix on the wall brings to mind the sacrificial love of Jesus, made powerfully evident in the Mass. The reconciliation room is a reminder of the healing power of forgiveness. The themes of the stained glass windows and the stations of the cross are reminders of the unconditional love of Christ. We need signs and symbols to help us focus upon deep truths of our faith and fathom something of their mystery.

Throughout the centuries the healings and miracles of Christ have remained a part of the collective faith of the Christian community. In the timelessness of God, experiences of faith and healing and acts of love still linger like fragrant incense in our churches, and contribute to the sense of God's presence.

Feeling at Home in Church

A woman said once that when she visited a Catholic church after many years of absence, she felt like she had truly "come home." As she sat in the back of the church in quiet prayer, just soaking up the atmosphere, she realized that the deep loneliness that had plagued her life for years, was actually a homesickness for God and the faith of her childhood. When she entered the church the prayerful environment had a drawing power that captured her heart again.

We are "at home" in our churches because of the presence of Jesus. Our churches are healing places because of the presence of Jesus. Perhaps you have been away from the Catholic Church for a period, and are exploring the possibility of coming home again. Or maybe you go to church, attend Mass and leave with little awareness that you have even been present. Perhaps it's just a routine to fulfill an obligation.

The Lord is inviting you to come to Him, to open to His healing love, to come and worship. There is a deep need in each of us to worship. You may find that the Lord will speak to you in His sacred place, and draw you into a powerful experience of healing through the holy sacrifice of the Mass.

Mary Ann's Story

Mary Ann Cortes was healed through the Mass. She spent seventeen years in mental hospitals in the New Orleans, Louisiana area, on every drug treatment program available for manic depressive patients except shock therapy. She encountered the healing Jesus during Mass, and over the course of several months was totally healed. The Lord took away the illness, and took away the fear, so that she could truly say, "I'm not afraid of the morning anymore." The Lord accomplished what no psychiatrist had been able to do. The testimony of her healing has deeply touched hundreds of lives.

"I am coming to know that the Eucharist is the greatest healing sacrament," Mary Ann says, "and that every Mass is a healing service. For seventeen years I was in and out of every mental hospital in the region of New Orleans, Louisiana. I was diagnosed as manic depressive and given almost every treatment available to psychiatric patients. The doctors gave up hope of my recovering my mental health, and doomed me to a life of mood- altering drugs. When I went to bed at night I would pray that I would die in my sleep, I was so afraid of waking up to another day of terror. After I was baptized in the Holy Spirit and began to attend healing Masses, I became mentally, emotionally and physically well. Today I am a new person in Christ. I'm not afraid of the morning anymore.

"In each Mass I unite all that I am with His sacrifice. In that union with Him I receive into my being the risen life of Jesus, which transforms me more and more. I identify with Him and receive His life. The more I actively participate in the Mass, the more real He becomes to me. Jesus Himself enters into me and heals me from the inside."

When Sister Rosemary Ford of South Dakota reviewed a draft of this book, she wrote the following comment about Mary Ann's story: "This is powerful. When someone who is severely depressed called me during my review of the text, I read the story to her over the phone. When I finished she was sobbing. It sounds just like me,' she cried. 'Do you think I will be healed too?' "

The Lord is healing His people today. The medical profession may have given up on you, or your loved one, but Jesus has not given up. He is here to heal you today. Come, receive Him in the Eucharist.

Healing Reflections

* In what places are you most open to God's healing love?

* Try to get in touch with the three most important healing aspects of these sacred places.

* What signs and symbols of faith are the most meaningful to you? Why?

Introduction to the Mass

Historically, the celebration of the Mass has been given many names, emphasizing different aspects of the observance. Scripture refers to it as the "Breaking of Bread" and "The Lord's Supper." The term "sacrifice" is also used, as well as "liturgy." The word "Mass" probably comes from *Ite missa est*, "Go, it is ended." The term that originally applied to dismissal came to be used in a broader sense. It has been suggested that the evolution came about because the term "Mass" became synonymous with "blessing."

Brendan Walsh of County Kerry, Ireland, shared the following story that deeply impressed upon him the timeless blessing of the Mass. In the introduction to his story he reflected, "When we enter Mass we step into a spiritual world, out of our time and into God's time. In God's timelessness Calvary extends across history, as present today in the Mass as it was 2,000 years ago, with all its healing effects. We are present with Mary and John at the foot of the cross. We are present with the crying mother in Cork City."

Brendan's Story

"A priest from New York, while celebrating a Mass in an auditorium in Cork City, Ireland in 1986, spoke about the healing power of Jesus in the Eucharist. He explained to the gathering of 1,000 people that Jesus

was wholly and completely present in the Eucharist,
and that in receiving His body and blood we should
expect to be healed of our illnesses. The priest
emphasized the need for Catholics to believe fully in
His presence, His power, and His desire to heal.

"During communion, sick and crippled people
began jumping out of their chairs. I saw with my own
eyes a mother crying as her baby's blindness was
cured. The newspapers reported stories of old women
jumping out of wheelchairs and many varied illnesses
cured.

"That was the first time I'd ever experienced
anything like that in my life. It deeply impressed
upon me the reality of the Eucharist as a healing
sacrament."

Covenant

To appreciate the power of the Mass we need to be
aware of how much God loves us. We need to
understand what He has done to prove that love. From
earliest times people have had trouble believing that
God loved them, and so he proved that love through a
series of covenants, first with Noah, then Abraham,
the nation of Israel (through Moses) and with David.
Each Old Testament covenant held increasingly
greater promises, leading up to the coming of Christ
and the beginning of the New Covenant. In every
covenant God took the initiative and established the
terms. Each reflected the love and the mercy of God,
and the unmerited favor extended to His people.

According to *Covenant in the Old Testament* by
Michael D. Guinan, O.F.M., a covenant is "...an
agreement or promise between two parties, solemnly
professed before witnesses and made binding by an
oath expressed verbally or by some symbolic action." [1]
Covenants generally have two parts: what the parties
agree to do; and the conditions we have to fulfill. The
promise creates an irrevocable partnership.

God followed the covenant form familiar to the
people. The procedure generally included the sacrifice

of an animal, such as a bull or a cow, which was split down the middle and separated into two pieces. Blood was shed because it was a symbol of life, so people were essentially saying, "We are putting our lives on the line." For example, consider two tribes—one strong in fighting and the other strong in education. Because they needed each other, they would enter into a covenant. At a meeting of the clans the leader of each tribe, the covenant representatives, would split the animal. Members of both tribes would stand around the animal while the two representatives walked in the blood between the two parts of the animal. This action symbolized putting their blood on the line. They would then stand in front of the people and make a covenant, pronouncing blessings on those who were faithful to the covenant and curses on those who broke the covenant. They would cut their wrists, tie them together, comingle their blood, and hold their bound hands up high in front of all the people, showing they were sealing the covenant with their blood.

Then the two leaders might exchange coats, as symbols of their power. In the light of this, it is interesting to reflect on Genesis 37. Joseph's father gave him a fine coat distinguished by its length and sleeves. This sign of favoritism roused his brothers' jealousy. It was the first episode that stirred up a hatred of Joseph, which ultimately led to their attempt to kill him lest he become too powerful. The exchange of coats has a psychological importance in covenants. As a part of completing the covenant the representatives would feed each other with bread and wine, the bread being a symbol of their bodies and the wine being symbols of their blood.

God's covenant with Abraham, Isaac, Moses and others throughout the Old Testament followed similar patterns. The Dogmatic Constitution on Divine Revelation in the *Documents of Vatican II* states: "In carefully planning and preparing the salvation of the whole human race, the God of supreme love...chose for Himself a person to whom He might entrust His promise. First He entered into a covenant with Abraham (Gen18:18) and, through Moses, with the people of Israel (Ex 24:8)." 2

God gave His Son, Jesus, as the sacrifice of the New Covenant. Jesus was our covenant meal and rose again to become our covenant representative. Through His Spirit, poured out as promised, He exchanged His strength for our weakness, His supply for our need, His health for our sickness. He gave us His name, His authority, His armor, His weapons.

Every time we receive Jesus in the Eucharist we are partaking of the covenant meal in sacramental form. Through the sacraments Jesus takes us beyond the visible (the water, the bread, the wine, the oil, the word, the touch) to the invisible. That invisible is pure love—Christ Himself, working through man.

Sacrifice

What greater way can a man demonstrate his love than to lay down his life for another? When a woman is pregnant she gives the child in her womb everything she has. All her life forces become involved in the growth of the unborn child. In a greater way the Lord gives us His very self in the Mass, saying, "I gave my life for you. All I have is available to nourish you and make you healthy and strong. All my resources are yours."

A powerful story came out in the newspapers about the 1988 Armenian earthquake that killed 50,000 people. In the collapse of an apartment building, Susanna Petrosyana and her four-year-old daughter, Gayaney, fell from the fifth floor to the basement and were pinned under wreckage, barely in reach of each other. Susanna discovered a 1-1/2 pound jar of blackberry jam nearby and on the second day gave the entire jar to Gayaney to eat. After awhile, when the jam was gone, the dehydrated child sobbed, "Mommy, I need to drink." Susanna later told reporters, "I thought my child was going to die of thirst...I had no water, no fruit juice, no liquids. It was then I remembered that I had my own blood." She found a piece of broken glass and began cutting her hand, and put it to her child's mouth. She knew she was going to die, but wanted her child to live. She doesn't remember what day she cut open her fingers, or how many times she used the method to feed her daughter. On the eighth day of their captivity they were found by rescue workers. This is a tremendous illustration of sacrifice.

Our lives as Christians involve daily sacrifice. We come to Mass primarily to sacrifice in union with the life and death of Jesus. As we sacrifice ourselves to God as a form of worship, we receive a blessing of conversion. In our repentance, our forgiveness, our renewal of the covenant, we grow in the ability to lay down our lives.

Knowing Jesus through Scripture

St. Jerome once said, "Ignorance of the scriptures is ignorance of Christ." The Mass is made up of two parts: the Liturgy of the Word, and the Liturgy of the Eucharist. The Church teaches that God is truly present in both parts of the liturgy. Through the scriptures, opened up through the light of the Holy Spirit, we come to know the Father, the Son and the Holy Spirit. Through study of scripture we come to know that Jesus teaches through healing, meeting people in their needs. If they are open, He touches them and heals them. If we don't know scripture, we won't be open to letting Jesus act in and through us in a similar way.

Father Paulissen's Story

Father Richard Paulissen's story is a good example of scripture coming to life under the anointing of the Holy Spirit.

"In the early days I learned how to say Mass in 12 minutes. I could talk on a retreat for three days and never refer to God. Then I went to the monastery in Pecos, New Mexico, and found myself in a Life in the Spirit seminar one night with 55 people, including seven Presbyterians and three priests. The Abbot prayed over me and I didn't feel a thing. I sat and watched people in different parts of the room singing three different songs, and it all seemed to fit.

"Then a long-haired boy of about 10 or 11 stood up, and I recalled the scripture, '...unless you change and become like little children you will not enter the kingdom of God' (Mt 18:3). The next thing I knew, I found myself standing in front of him asking for prayer for the baptism in the Holy Spirit. After prayer I sat down again, feeling nothing. I said, 'Well, you know, God, I'm really tough. I don't need this. I can get through life in pain. I've been in agony up to now; I can keep on.'

"Then I looked down and saw a book called *Good News for Modern Man.* When I picked it up I discovered it was the New Testament. It fell open to the Gospel of Luke, and I began reading it aloud. I had studied scripture for eight years, but it never sounded like this. The parables became my life story. When I got to the 24th chapter of Luke I came to the verse, '...Why do you search for the living one among the dead?' (Lk 24:5). The word 'living' exploded in me for the first time, running through me from head to foot. He is alive! He lives! He lives! I had been worshipping a dead God, and that had been my trouble. I had been worshipping a history-book God, not the living Lord Jesus! 'He lives! He lives!' kept running through my mind. I had an incredible sense of someone's presence beside me, very close. I said, 'Jesus!' That night He came into my life, and I was never, never to be the same." (Father Richard Paulissen, Houston, Texas)

Healing Promises in Scripture

As we study the scriptures we are reminded of our loving Father's great healing promises. Often in the New Testament it is stated, "Jesus healed them all." Consider some works of Jesus, as reflected in the following scriptures:

> *...They carried to Him all those afflicted with various diseases and racked with pain: the possessed, the lunatics, the paralyzed. He cured them all.* (Mt 4:24)

> *Many people followed him and he cured them all...* (Mt 12:16)

> *The blind and the lame came to him inside the temple area and he cured them.* (Mt 21:14)

> *...and He healed all who were in need of healing.* (Lk 9:11)

A prayerful study of scripture will draw us into the knowledge of God as a loving, blessing Father with gifts of healing for all.

Healing Reflections

* Think about the time you first entered into a covenant with your Heavenly Father.

* When is the last time you renewed that covenant?

* What does sacrifice mean to you?

Miracles through the Sacraments

Morton Kelsey in *Psychology, Medicine and Christian Healing* challenges us to expect healing through the sacraments. We have in our Church, he reminds us, "...the same basic sacramental approach to it (healing) as Jesus. Some word, a touch, or a material element such as oil was believed to convey the power of the Spirit that was channeled through the Christian. The words and touch were important as outward and visible signs of an inner grace, a spiritual energy. The sacramental acts were only outward carriers of the Spirit that wished to heal." [1]

Healing through the sacraments is very real to Father Richard Woldum of Los Angeles, California. Shortly after his ordination he was assigned for one year as a hospital chaplain at St. Joseph's Hospital in Alton, Illinois. He knew nothing about healing, but was soon to learn of its reality through the power of the sacraments. He shares about his experiences with one patient in the following story.

"One morning I received a call to come to the emergency room to see an 11-year-old boy named Johnny who was dying. I found him on a breathing machine, his head swollen very large.

"Johnny's parents told me that he had been riding his bike on a gravel road near his home when a truck came flying over the hill and hit him head-on. The collision caused him to be thrown into the nearby field. When the ambulance arrived the medics found his head cut wide open with half his brains scattered in the field. They literally picked up pieces of his brain, shoved them into his head, and took him to the hospital.

"When I asked Johnny's parents if he had been baptized, they said, 'No.' They informed me they attended no church but prayed at home as a family. I asked them if they would like me to baptize Johnny. They glanced at each other as if to say, 'It couldn't cause any harm,' then said to me, 'Go ahead.' They also said if I wanted to I could baptize him into the Catholic faith. That night, with the parents and two nurses as witnesses, I baptized Johnny.

"The next morning I was doing communion rounds when my beeper went off. Johnny's doctor wanted me in the intensive care unit. 'What you do last night?' he asked in broken English, as I met him outside Johnny's room. I explained to the doctor, a Buddhist, that I had baptized Johnny (with the permission of his parents) so that he could go to heaven. When I asked him why he was so concerned, he informed me that the boy's swelling had disappeared. The doctor was still convinced that the boy would die, however; or if he lived, remain a vegetable, never moving, talking or even moving his eyes.

"That night Johnny's parents thanked me for baptizing him. I then explained about the anointing of the sick, and asked if they would like Johnny to receive that sacrament. With their agreement and in their presence, I anointed Johnny.

"The next morning during communion rounds the doctor again paged me on my beeper. He met me at the door of intensive care and directed me to Johnny's room, explaining on the way that he had heard from the nurses that I had again prayed for Johnny.

"Then he pointed to Johnny's eyes and asked, 'What you do?' I saw that Johnny's eyes were moving. 'It was just the power of Jesus through prayers for the sick,' I responded. He gave a faintly sarcastic grin and said, 'It no matter. Boy no talk or move. He remain vegetable.'

"It was now the third night, counting the night of the accident. I suggested to the parents that they permit me to give Johnny the sacrament of confirmation. They agreed.

"The following morning his legs and arms were moving. The doctor said to me in front of the parents, 'I no longer in control.' He was simply unable to explain what was happening. The parents turned to me and said they wanted to become Catholics. I recommended that they wait and see what happened to Johnny before making a final decision.

"That evening when I explained to them about the Eucharist, they said they wanted this for Johnny too. I gave him some Precious Blood through an eye dropper. The next morning he was making sounds.

"The weekend was now upon me. It was Labor Day 1979 and I went home to celebrate my grandmother's 90th birthday. When I checked in on Johnny upon my return, I learned he had been transferred to the third floor, which was the surgery unit. I went upstairs to see him, fearing that he had gone back to surgery. He was sitting on his bed, talking to his mother.

"After his recovery they took another x-ray of his head and found that the part of his brain that had spilled out into the field had grown back.

"When I eventually talked to Johnny's parents about becoming Catholics, they informed me they would continue praying at home. The doctor in the case started looking into Christianity. Three nurses converted to Catholicism."

Healing Reflections

* If you witnessed powerful healing through the sacraments how would your reception of the sacraments change?

* What three things in Johnny's story touched you the most?

PART II

INTRODUCTORY RITES

Introductory Rite

As you enter the church, consider the grace of God that brought you to this present moment. Do you remember when you first said, "Jesus, You are Lord of my life?" Father Richard Paulissen's testimony continues as he reflects on this grace: "I have asked the Lord ten thousand times, 'Lord, why did it take me so long to discover You in my life? The fullness, the joy, the peace, the love.' When I read about Peter in the scriptures I didn't feel so self-condemning. He walked hand-in-hand with Jesus; he was the rock upon which Jesus chose to build His Church. The scriptures tell us that Peter was amazed when he saw the empty tomb. It just shows you that we are all human. Even Peter was amazed."

Jesus is infinitely patient with our slow learning and continues to draw us to Himself. He brings us now to this most sacred time of Eucharistic union with Him.

An Investment

Invest in this moment. You have made a covenant with Jesus, who loves you so very much. Enter in, and deepen your knowledge of this truth. Immerse yourself in the reality of God's gift. Expect great things. Mary Constancio of Slayton, Texas, exhorts people to open their hearts to the transforming power of God through the Mass. In her reports of contact with the Blessed Mother, Mary says: "I have seen the Blessed Mother at Mass on a number of occasions. She really loves the

Mass. I have seen her kneeling and adoring Christ and praying near the altar. When I go to Mass it is no longer for me just another passing time; it is always a conversion experience. I feel great love from our Heavenly Father at that time."

Invest in this moment. God loves you: every part of the Mass proclaims this truth. He wants your openness to His love, not your performance. He is inviting you to participate, in whatever way you can.

Come to Mass early and get in tune with the Lord. Like athletes warm up before a game, prayer is our "warm up" before Mass. If we come in ice cold and not in tune, it's easy to become ritualistic. Ask the Lord to prepare your heart to hear His word. Read the scriptures for the Mass ahead of time so when they are proclaimed you will hear them in your heart. Be attentive to the specific word of love Jesus will say to you during Mass. Invest in this moment. It will never pass this way again.

Holy Water

When we enter church we sign ourselves with holy water, blessed by a priest to heal us, and to expel demons. There have been reports of people being healed as they blessed themselves with holy water. A man in Mobile, Alabama woke up with a burning eye and asked his wife for some Murine. Discovering that it was all gone, she passed him the holy water instead. He applied it to the distressed eye and was instantly healed. "The pain is gone!" he exclaimed.

St. Teresa of Avila and many other saints advise the use of holy water. People have come to me with a sense of evil in their homes and I have given them holy water to use. Afterward they report a new sense of peace. Using holy water in church should encourage families to use it daily in the home. I know of a couple who bless their house in the morning and evening with holy water. A nursing supervisor of the operating room in a hospital blesses the facility every morning with holy water and is convinced that it makes the day go more peacefully. Even doctors will come and ask her to bless them with holy water when things are going wrong. Expect the Lord to bless you deeply when you sign yourself with holy water.

This is a powerful sacramental of the Church. The prayer for the blessing of holy water says:

> *God our Father, Your gift of water brings life and freshness to the earth; it washes away our sins and brings us eternal life. We ask You now to bless this water, and to give us Your protection on this day which You have made Your own. Renew the living spring of Your life within us and protect us in spirit and body, that we may be free from sin and come into Your presence to receive Your gift of salvation. We ask this through Christ our Lord.*
>
> *Amen.*

The water is blessed for healing and deliverance from everything harmful, unclean, hurtful and not of the kingdom of God.

The Sign of the Cross

The Mass begins. "In the name of the Father, and of the Son, and of the Holy Spirit." The sign of the cross is a sign of hope that summarizes our faith: in the name of our loving Heavenly Father who created us; in the name of Jesus, sent to redeem and to heal; in the name of the Holy Spirit, who is continually sanctifying us.

We begin Mass by announcing that we have come in the name of the Father, the Son and the Holy Spirit. To come "in His name" means we come into His presence, linked to His nature, identified with Him, exercising His power. We have the authority of His name, in much the same way that we might have the authority of the president, or the king. As Christians we come under the name and authority of the King of Kings, making the sign of the cross as our royal birthmark.

Jesus died as our substitute and gave us the right to use the name given to Him. He told His disciples to go in His name—that they had His authority and His power. From earliest times the Church has taught us that in His name we are armed against the powers of evil and can perform signs and wonders.

There is power in the name of Jesus. Philippians 2:9-11 reminds us that God exalted Jesus to the highest place, and "...bestowed on Him the name above every other name, so that at Jesus' name every knee must bend in the heavens, on the earth and under the earth, and every tongue proclaim to the glory of God the Father: JESUS CHRIST IS LORD!"

We begin in the presence of the Lord Jesus Christ, in the power of His name. That power is love.

> *The grace of our Lord Jesus Christ and the love of God and the fellowship of the Holy Spirit be with you all.* (2Cor13:13)

The grace of our Lord Jesus Christ...Grace is free and unmerited favor. *The Church's Confession of Faith* states: "Fundamentally, grace means that we are unconditionally accepted, affirmed, and loved by God through Jesus Christ in the Holy Spirit and that we are wholly one with Him in this love. Grace is personal communion and friendship with God, personal participation in the life of God...a life rooted in grace means a life rooted in faith, hope and love." [1]

Evelyn Byrd Fagan of Santa Rosa, California, experienced the grace of God in her conversion experience after her son's suicide: "I had been a non-believer for 45 years. Then my twenty-year-old son, John, took his life by jumping off the Golden Gate bridge in San Francisco, California. It was the worst agony of my life. I couldn't function. I went to a medical doctor and then a psychiatrist for medication, but woke up the next morning knowing that pills were not what I needed. I got on my knees and cried out to God my Father. I hadn't thought about Him for years. Like the prodigal son, I was received by my Heavenly

Father with an abundance of love and blessings and grace. My whole life was transformed. Through the worst agony in my life, came the greatest blessing." "So let us confidently approach the throne of grace to receive mercy and favor and to find help in time of need" (Heb4:16).

and the love of God... Do we have a clear understanding of God as a loving Father? As a healing Father? After twenty-five years of Catholic education I still considered God as judge until the Spirit touched me. Then I began to see God more as a loving Father. Perhaps during the Introductory Rite of the Mass we could ask for healing of any negative attitudes that may have developed through the years toward God as a loving Father. Those attitudes might include, "God sends sickness," or "God wants me to have this problem." You may have come to Mass with physical or emotional pain. Our Father wants to heal you in body, mind and spirit. He wants to heal hurts, guilt, fear, suicidal tendencies, compulsions, addictions, hearts, neuritis, bursitis, backaches and headaches. He wants us to bring all our spiritual, psychological and physical needs to Him for healing.

Many people have an unconscious fear of God, believing if they love the Lord and get too close to Him, He will make them suffer. Those thoughts are inconsistent with the idea of a loving Father. Primarily these hidden fears grew out of a religious education that taught a theology of suffering; therefore people tend to associate religion with suffering.

Father Ralph Weishaar, O.F.M., upon reading the above statement, suggests that something should be said to acknowledge suffering, the cross, pain, "The sorrowful mysteries," as a normal and expected part of the Christian life. "Holiness involves pain," he reflects, "but it is pain 'allowed' by God, and, having meaning and purpose."

Perhaps it's a matter of emphasis. The saints suffered, yet experienced a tremendous sense of closeness, warmth, and love of the Father, Jesus Christ and the Holy Spirit. Yet we tend to look at their suffering more than their intimate love relationship with God. When we accentuate the negative instead of affirming the good, our relationship with God can be adversely affected.

The Church's Confession of Faith states: The "...message that God is boundless love is the very heart of what Jesus says about God...The conviction existed in the Church from the very beginning that what is properly and specifically Christian is an intimate personal communion with God, in knowing oneself to be a child, a son or daughter of God." [2]

Many people have difficulty opening up to God as loving Father because of a poor relationship with an earthly Father. Because Doris Deutsch in the following story was abandoned by her earthly father, it was hard for her to know God as loving Father. When you read her story, ask the Lord to heal any negativity in your relationship with your earthly father that would be a barrier to knowing God as loving Father.

Doris' Story

"My father abandoned his wife and four children when I was young. I never saw him and never heard from him and until I was 18 I believed he was dead. When Aunt Emma, my father's sister, told me he was alive, I was astonished. I gave her my graduation picture to give to him, and hoped he would contact me. He never did. Later, when I committed my life to Jesus, I developed a relationship with Him and knew His love. Yet I was afraid of God the Father. Knowing Him as a tender and loving Father seemed impossible.

"One day I learned that my father had died. My deepest prayer to meet him would not be fulfilled. I felt an enormous hurt, and visited Aunt Emma. She told me a little about his life and death, and said he decided not to see me because he was too ashamed of his behavior as a young father. He must have known, through her, that for 17 years I had asked about him.

"I stood near his grave engulfed in anguish. My search was over. This was as close as I would ever get to my father. I cried out to God, 'It's too late, too late! I have no father!' At that point I heard a voice say, 'I am your Father.' I turned around but no one was there. Again I heard the words, this time softer. 'I am your Father.' It was hard to believe at first, but the God I had feared spoke to me. I felt His love surround me, and I was suddenly able to understand the meaning of the verse, 'Then God's own peace, which is beyond all understanding, will stand guard over your hearts and minds, in Christ Jesus' (Phil4:7).

"Because God revealed Himself to me as Father, I no longer feel the hurt of an abandoned child, nor the pain from my fruitless search. I was healed so that only the memory and none of the pain remains. That afternoon in the lonely cemetery changed my life. Where God was once only a remote figure of the Trinity, He is now the Father I talk with, walk with, and praise each day. I realize this wonderful Father loves all His children so much that He impatiently awaits the day that He can draw us close to Himself forever." [3]

Something very deep in Doris' life was affirmed that day. An old struggle was ended, an old issue was resolved, and she received the fathering that she needed.

and the fellowship of the Holy Spirit be with you all... *The Church's Confession of Faith* states, "...friendship with God takes effect in different ways. It shows itself in man himself. The Holy Spirit heals and sanctifies him. He sanctifies him by joining him to God, making him whole and entire. The Spirit brings about order, discipline and moderation in man...The Spirit also brings about friendship and communion with Jesus Christ...Because communion with God is the deepest fulfillment of man, whoever opens himself to the working of the Spirit will be filled with deep inner peace, with consolation and joy." [4]

Through the Holy Spirit we have access to Jesus, who takes us to the Father. The Holy Spirit is sometimes described as the "revealed love of Father and Son." Through Him we experience the love of God in a tangible way. As we yield our lives to the management of the Holy Spirit, He brings enlightenment of Jesus into our spirits. He helps us understand ourselves and shows us how to live.

Those who yield to the ministry of the Holy Spirit, allowing His love to soak into the very roots of their being, find deep healing in primary relationships with God, self and parents. Most of us try to do things on our own, instead of allowing the Spirit of God to do them through us. When we simply rest in Him and let Him be what we need, we find healing and peace beyond measure.

"And also with you."

God calls us to respond to His love. Think about the most beautiful Mass you ever attended. What was it that struck you about that Mass? How did God's grace touch you at that moment? Why did His grace touch you at that moment? Ask the Lord to bring back some of the joy of that moment, that you may enter into future Masses with more openness and expectancy.

Take home and apply what you learned at Mass. Ask yourself, "What one thing touched me the most in Mass today?" Build on that response, study that word, that idea, that scripture verse, in the coming week. Let it be an occasion for dialogue with the Lord.

The effects of the Mass are brought about in large part by the faith-filled response of the community, encouraged and sparked by the priest. It's a team effort that brings forth the power of God in the community. When we say, "And also with you," let's use it as an opportunity to step forward and get involved. This opens us up for healing.

Survey Responses

The survey respondents were asked, "What was your greatest healing at Mass?" Some of those responses include:

* Conversion experience at a New Year's Eve Mass. (Pete Smith)

* Healing of an emotional scar so deep that I don't know its exact cause; only that it no longer exists. (Mary Kohn)

* When my heart knew, absolutely knew, that God was MY Father. My mind always knew, but my heart didn't. (Jacqueline Roberts)

* Forgiveness of my only child because she married without my knowledge. (Carmen Sale)

* At a healing conference the Lord gave me a very important word about an inner hurt He was going to heal. This hurt was so deeply buried that I had not been able to discover it in more than 25 years of psychiatry and inner healing. The healing was probably made possible by the fact that I was able to get to Mass every morning for five months prior to the healing conference. (legal assistant)

* Forgiveness of my ex-husband for his abuse of the children. (Donna L.)

* My severe migraine left after the Body and Blood of Christ were elevated. (Ann Belale)

* Overcoming depression after becoming a widow. (Lillian Crow)

* After the ending of a relationship that was quite painful to break off, my Lord came to me after communion as if with a surgeon's hand. He entered my heart and scraped it out as if cleansing the woundedness. I cried because it hurt emotionally but felt uplifted afterward. (Jerilyn Gravois)

* I was under chiropractic care for sciatica—pinched nerve—and the pain was often excruciating for nearly a year. When my wife said, "You don't need the

doctor, Jesus will heal you," I prayed, "Jesus, now it's your turn." Within two or three days the condition cleared and hasn't recurred for over a year. (Edward Popielarski)

In the Introductory Rite we have the opportunity to enter into a deeper appreciation of the Father's healing love, remembering that "God is love" (1Jn 4:16). As a loving Father He desires for us to receive and enter into His love. Let's seek to be open to receive His love as we begin the Mass in His name.

Healing Reflections

* What would your life be like without Sunday Mass, or daily Mass?

* Capture the feelings of the most meaningful Mass you ever attended.

* How do you prepare for Mass?

* Reflect on three ways you can apply what you learn in Mass.

* Does a poor relationship with your earthly father interfere with your relationship with your Heavenly Father?

* Write a letter to your Heavenly Father expressing the changes you would like in that relationship.

Penitential Rite

As we prepare to celebrate the mystery of Christ's love, let us acknowledge our failures and ask the Lord for pardon and strength.

In preparation for the Penitential Rite, visualize yourself sitting quietly in a favorite place, contemplating your relationship with the Lord. Is there something in your heart that holds back the full force of His love? Are there barriers that block the flow of grace? How have you not loved yourself? Ask the Lord, "What is blinding me to Your love? Why can't I love myself the way You love me?"

Most of us can think of dozens of negative qualities about ourselves, but few positive attributes. Most of us have difficulty with self-love. Psalm 139 says, "I am fearfully and wonderfully made." We argue, "How can that be?" Our Heavenly Father says, "But you ARE wonderfully made—imperfect, limited, dysfunctional, deprived of love, yes, but fearfully and wonderfully made."

Instead of accepting this truth, we accept a lie in its place. There is a poignant story about a little boy named Steven who was kidnapped and molested for seven years. When he was returned to his parents he was filled with guilt, certain that he was responsible for all the bad that had happened. He needed to be released into a knowledge of his worth. We need to be released into a knowledge of our worth.

As you confess to God your weaknesses and failures, ask Him for insights about why you do the things you do. Be patient with yourself. The more you

grow in the Spirit, the more you will see your
weaknesses, faults and failings in the light of His
mercy and love. Patience brings humility and poverty
of spirit, which opens the door to God's grace. When we
know we can't do it on our own, then the Lord can
work. When we know His mercy, then we can be open
about our weaknesses. When we can lay our
weaknesses before Him, we are wide open to receive His
healing grace.

> *I confess to almighty God, and to you my*
> *brothers and sisters, that I have sinned through*
> *my own fault in my thoughts and in my words, in*
> *what I have done and in what I have failed to do;*
> *and I ask blessed Mary, ever virgin, all the angels*
> *and saints, and you, my brothers and sisters, to*
> *pray for me to the Lord our God.*

As we begin the Penitential Rite let's remember
that it is only by an action of the Holy Spirit in our
hearts that we can say, "I believe my Heavenly Father
truly forgives me for the wrongs I have done." It is only
by His grace that we can say, "Lord, I receive Your
forgiveness."

Because He has forgiven us, we can forgive others.
The Penitential Rite is the key to healing through the
Mass because it is here that we open ourselves to
receive the forgiveness of the Lord, and reach out to
forgive ourselves and others.

Many people say they have no need to forgive. It
has been my experience, however, that we all need to
forgive. We may need to forgive ourselves for
unconscious resentment toward God for hurts, pains,
death of a loved one or unanswered prayer. We
need ongoing forgiveness in our father/mother
relationships, with sisters, brothers, relatives and
marriage partners. Parents need to forgive their
children for being out of fellowship in the Church. A
woman said to me one time, "Father, I never realized
that I had not forgiven my son for marrying a Mormon
girl and leaving the Church to become an active

Mormon. After your talk I was able to forgive him." We need to forgive co-workers. People in management say that keeping peace among employees is one of their most important and difficult problems. Employers, employees, neighbors and church people need to be forgiven. Within the Catholic Church we may need to forgive bishops, priests, nuns, parish council members and lay leaders. We may need to forgive professional people: doctors, nurses, lawyers, judges, teachers. We may need to forgive friends.

Who is the one person in life who has hurt you the most? If you can't think of anyone, ask the Holy Spirit to reveal the person by name. Take a pencil and paper and write down the names of people who have hurt you that you still need to forgive.

I encourage you to pray the following *Forgiveness Prayer* regularly for nine days—or even weeks, months and years. People with degenerative illnesses should consider saying the prayer on an on-going basis, since the roots of many diseases may be related to bitterness, resentment and unforgiveness.

As you continue to pray this prayer, buried memories will gently flow up into your consciousness to be released into the love of God. As they emerge, simply give them to the Lord. Forgiveness is a decision, not a feeling. If we give forgiveness from our will, God will give it to us from our hearts.

Also, when we forgive we are not admitting that others are right and we are wrong. We are not saying that we weren't hurt. We are not denying the other person's responsibility or accountability. As we forgive injustices we are simply deciding to obey God. We are not allowing the wrongs of another to dictate our attitudes, actions and emotions. We are taking charge of them.

Something wonderful will happen as you surrender to this healing process. God is going to open your heart and empower you with new vitality, new energy and new health. As you repent and forgive, you are perhaps at that moment most completely united with Jesus. You enter into the miraculous realm of

God's love. You are truly set free. Forgiveness is love in action.

Muriel Neveux, R.N., of Lawrence, Massachusetts, had a powerful vision during Mass one time that she shares with you here. I pray that this experience of healing through forgiveness will be helpful to you.

Muriel's Meditation

"I was standing beneath the cross gazing upon Jesus in His agony. He looked down on me and asked me to bring to the cross each person who had harmed me in any way. I looked at him skeptically, not wanting to do this. He said, 'Bring them to me and forgive as I have forgiven you.' When I did this, I brought many people to the foot of the cross. It was like a parade. At one point, one of the persons I wanted to bring wouldn't come. I turned to the Lord on the cross and asked for His help. He came down from the cross and walked over to the person with His arms outstretched. She began to pound on His chest with clenched fists. The more she did this the harder His arms embraced her, until finally she accepted the power of His love in that embrace. He then put one arm around her shoulder and one around my shoulder and walked us to the cross. At the foot of the cross He took her hand and my hand and made us clasp them with His. We could feel His healing love penetrating us. After we were reconciled He then took His place upon the cross again, looked down on all of us, smiled and said, 'I am here on the cross to set you free. I have redeemed you. You are new people with hearts of flesh.' Then he looked up toward heaven and said, 'It is finished.' "

As you stand before God angry and hurt, perhaps longing for revenge (but wanting even more to be in God's perfect will), I pray that you will have the courage to release all bitterness and hatred and choose to love with God's love.

Forgiveness Prayer

Lord Jesus Christ, I ask for the grace today to forgive everyone in my life. I know that You will give me strength to forgive. I let go of all resentment toward You because of hardships, death and sickness in the family. I surrender to You today in faith and trust; You love me more than I love myself, and want my happiness more than I desire it for myself. Jesus, You are Lord of my life. Please come into my heart in a deeper way and remove anything that would block the flow of Your love. Please give me the grace to rest in Your arms and allow myself to be loved by You.

Lord, because You have forgiven me, I can forgive MYSELF for sins, faults and failings. For all that is truly bad in myself or all that I think is bad, I do forgive myself. For any delving into the occult, ouija boards, horoscopes, seances, fortune telling or using lucky charms; for any calling upon sources of power apart from You; for taking Your name in vain; for not worshiping You; for hurting my parents; for getting drunk or using drugs; for sins against my purity; for adultery; for abortion; for stealing or lying; I truly forgive myself today. I let go of all self-directed negativity. I release the things held against myself and make peace with myself today.

I now stand before You as an intercessor and extend forgiveness to my ANCESTORS for acts of negativity and unlove. I come before You, Lord, on behalf of everyone in my family tree and apologize for any sinful actions. Let forgiveness flow through my family tree. Let the wounds of the past be healed through my act of forgiveness today. Thank You, Lord.

I forgive my MOTHER, Lord. I forgive her for times she may have hurt me, resented me or punished me unfairly. I forgive her for preferring my brothers and sisters; I forgive her for telling me I was dumb, ugly, stupid, the worst of the children, or that I cost the family a lot of money. I forgive her for rejecting me, abandoning me, or attempting to abort me. I forgive her for telling me I was unwanted, an accident, or a mistake. I forgive her for any lack of nurturing, lack of hugs and kisses. For any ways she did not provide a deep, satisfying mother's blessing I truly forgive her today. I pray for her today, and ask God's blessing upon her.

I forgive my FATHER. I forgive him for any non-support, lack of companionship, drinking, severe punishments, sexual abuse, desertion or unfaithfulness to my mother. I forgive him for not showing his love; lack of hugs and kisses, tenderness and intimacy. For any ways that I did not receive a deep, satisfying father's blessing I do forgive him today. I pray for him today, and ask God's blessing upon him.

I forgive my SISTERS and BROTHERS for any acts of unlove and negativity. I forgive those who rejected me, lied about me, resented me, physically harmed me, or competed for my parents' love. I forgive all BLOOD RELATIVES for harm done to our family. I forgive all IN-LAWS for any abuses and expressions of negativity and unlove. I pray for them and ask God's blessing upon them.

I forgive my SPOUSE for lack of love, lack of affection, lack of consideration, lack of support, or lack of communication; I forgive my spouse for faults, failings and weaknesses. I ask God's blessing on my spouse today.

I forgive my CHILDREN today. I forgive them for lack of respect, lack of obedience, lack of love, lack of attention, lack of understanding. I forgive them for their bad habits, for falling away from the Church, for any action that disturbed me. I pray for them and ask God's blessing upon them.

I forgive my FRIENDS. I forgive them for letting me down, gossiping about me, borrowing money and not returning it, and encouraging sinful behavior. I pray for them and ask God's blessing upon them.

I forgive my NEIGHBORS. For any act of negativity, for lack of consideration, for prejudice, for running down the neighborhood, I do forgive them today. I pray for them and ask God's blessing upon them.

I forgive PRIESTS, NUNS, BISHOPS AND THE POPE for lack of support, lack of friendliness, pettiness, bad sermons, for any hurt they may have inflicted. I pray for them and ask God's blessing upon them.

I forgive my EMPLOYER. I forgive him for not paying me enough money, for not appreciating my work, for being unkind and unreasonable, for being angry or unfriendly, for not promoting me, for not complimenting me on my work. I pray for my employer today and ask God's blessing on him.

I forgive all PROFESSIONAL people. I forgive LAWYERS for any harm they may have done. I forgive SCHOOL TEACHERS for humiliating me and imposing unfair punishments; for lack of warmth; for not encouraging my potential. I forgive DOCTORS, NURSES and other MEDICAL PROFESSIONALS for treating me unjustly. I pray for them and ask God's blessing upon them.

I forgive people in PUBLIC SERVICE. I forgive those who passed laws opposing Christian values. I forgive POLICEMEN for any abuses. I pray for them today and ask God's blessing upon them.

Heavenly Father, I now forgive every member of SOCIETY who has hurt me in any way. I forgive those who have rejected me or hurt me by criminal action, sexual aggression or obscene actions. I forgive the strangers and nameless perpetrators of evil in society. I forgive those who have defrauded me or defamed my character. I forgive those to whom I cannot go directly and face with my anger: the burglar who got away, the rapist, the murderer, unknown carriers of disease, wartime aggressors. I pray for them today and ask God's blessing upon them.

Heavenly Father, I now forgive by an act of my will, the ONE PERSON IN LIFE WHO HAS HURT ME THE MOST. The one who is the hardest to forgive, I now choose to forgive. I also make peace with the one family member, the one friend, and the one member of the clergy who has hurt me the most in

**life. I pray for them today, and ask God's blessing
on them. Thank You, Heavenly Father, for setting us
free. In Jesus' name. Amen.**

If you now feel better, then you have just experienced
healing through forgiveness. You should feel lighter and
much more peaceful. Forgiveness is an act of the will,
not the emotions. As you choose to forgive, God will empower that choice and bring it, in time, from your head
to your heart.

I recommend that you pray this prayer daily, perhaps for nine days as a novena. Ask the Holy Spirit
to open your heart to deeper levels of forgiveness. It
also would help to read books on forgiveness.[1] This
will heighten your awareness of the need to forgive and
increase your "forgiveness consciousness."

Survey Respondents Share Forgiveness Stories

* I had stopped receiving the Lord for about two years
  since a former co-worker made my life miserable to
  the point of quitting my job. I couldn't forgive myself,
  and didn't feel worthy of receiving the Lord. During a
  seminar on healing of self-image in 1987 at St. Mary's
  Cathedral in San Francisco I found out how much the
  Lord loves me. I was able to forgive the other person
  and myself, then was able finally to receive Jesus in
  the Eucharist. (A.E.)

* I was able to forgive big hurts in my marriage and love
  my husband to a greater degree. (Frances Y.)

* When I was almost dead of brokenness due to family
  relationships, I went to Mass and saw Jesus extending His hands to me as if saying, "Forgive them as I
  forgave you." (Leticia Cadiz)

* In 1987 Father Robert DeGrandis walked into the
  Lady of Peace Cathedral in Hawaii at noon Mass.
  We had not expected him until the night service. As
  he commenced Mass I felt a strange shooting pain

from my neck to one shoulder, followed by a quick pain to the other shoulder where I had bursitis two years previously. Intermittent little pains continued throughout Mass. As I walked home after Mass the darting pains became stronger, and moved to my spine. At home I rested on the floor. I had arthritis for 32 years, apparently tied into my unforgiveness of my first husband. I thought I had forgiven him, but I had, instead, 'blanked him out.' The healing process lasted five hours. By the time Father DeGrandis started the scheduled healing Mass that evening I was already healed. Father Bob was not near me at any time. (Marguerite Bilger)

* The most meaningful Mass I ever attended was with a priest-friend. I was filled with anger, hatred and unforgiveness in my heart toward family members. I couldn't even reach out at the Sign of Peace. When he recited the *Forgiveness Prayer* I was lifted out of my darkness and brought into the light. At communion I was filled with love and forgiveness. All resentment and anger was gone. I relived my life and was able to forgive all who hurt me the most. (Mattie Hyatt)

The Sacrament of Reconciliation

When we enter the confessional after forgiving our neighbor we fulfill the requirements laid down in scripture: to forgive our neighbor; to confess to one another; to seek forgiveness from God for offenses committed against His love. The confessional is set in a public place and the presence of the priest through whom God administers absolution represents not only Christ but all the people of God.

A psychiatrist spoke one time of patients who needed to pour out their worries, frustrations and sins. She said that such a convenience cost her patients a lot of money. When it was suggested to her that the Catholic confessional had served this purpose for centuries, she was fascinated by the truth of that statement. Another psychologist said he could release

90% of his patients if they would forgive! When we use the confessional with the right disposition we reap spiritual, physical and emotional blessings.

Survey Responses

In the survey we asked 100 people the question, "How often do you receive the sacrament of reconciliation?" The following responses were given:

Never	1
More than once a week	1
Weekly	2
Twice a month	6
Three times a month	2
Monthly	18
1-3 months	25
3-6 months	1
6-12 months	9
Annually	3
Variable times	12
Not answered	25

A survey respondent stated that he goes to the sacrament of reconciliation twice a month as "medicine for his spirit." He had lived a very rough life and had done many things for which he was very sorry. He went through a major spiritual conversion and was deeply changed, yet knew the old patterns still had a certain pull. The "medicine for his spirit" enabled him consistently to make healthy choices and avoid the old patterns.

I encourage each of you to make the sacrament of reconciliation a regular part of your Christian life. We need these gifts and graces, given by God to keep us strong and healthy and connected to Him.

May almighty God have mercy on us, forgive
us our sins, and bring us to everlasting life. Amen.

Sister Eileen's Story

Sister Eileen Jones is a member of the Victorian Congregation of Sisters of the Presentation of the Blessed Virgin Mary, living in Victoria, Australia. Her story began in 1956 when she fell down a flight of stairs and damaged her spine. It is a powerful testimony of God's grace. She has given us permission to share her story.

"Through a misunderstanding I waited three months after my fall for a hospital bed. When a doctor eventually put me in traction I later learned that it was not handled properly. A series of events followed because of the error that kept deteriorating my condition. The prognosis was that I would eventually end up in a wheelchair on pain medication for the rest of my life. I eventually lost the use of my right side, then was told following a hearing test that I was going deaf. My eyes also began to deteriorate. I had a hysterectomy because of the traction error, and was finally sent to a psychiatrist. My medication, 27 tablets a day, did not deaden the pain. My mobility continued to deteriorate. By March 1977 I could not stretch my hands beyond my knees. To make things worse, some of my former superiors didn't believe anything was wrong with me.

"One day at a directed retreat a priest came to me and said, 'Eileen we are going to pray about your back, and when it is healed it will be like a line of white fire burning through every nerve of your spinal system and bringing it back to life.' He prayed for me every day on the retreat. On the fourth day I said to him, 'Do you know, I can forgive all my previous superiors who did not believe that anything was wrong with me?' He replied, 'Eileen, the Lord can now heal your spine.' I could forgive, so now our Lord could heal. By His grace I had allowed the block to be removed.

"Sunday during the first reading of the Mass I felt my neck being jerked as though a chiropractor was putting it in place. I suddenly realized I could turn my head from side to side, which I had not been able to do for two years. At the Prayer of the Faithful the priest thanked the Lord for the most tremendous experience of his life. (I learned later he was referring to my healing.) The next morning the priest said, 'The Lord is healing your spine in three sections.' (It was injured in three sections.) As he prayed that day I saw little white electric globes connected by fine wire, all lighting up one by one. It still did not dawn on me that my spine was healed. In the afternoon in chapel it suddenly occurred to me that I was sitting in an ordinary chair, upright, with no pain. I wept before the Lord as I realized my back was healed, and knelt for the first time in eleven years.

"During the night I couldn't sleep because the nerves in my right leg and hip were coming back to life and the leg was growing to its right length. When the sun came up I could see everything in my room clearly, without glasses. I heard my watch tick for the first time in seven years.

"When I told the priest he smiled and said, 'And there will be a lot more healing. If your Lord had totally healed you in an instant you might have had a breakdown. Eileen, He has been very gentle with you.' The Lord can do so much more than we could ever ask or imagine.

"One day a woman to whom I had been ministering asked me to tell her the story of my healing. I inadvertently mentioned the name of the first doctor who set up the traction improperly. When she heard the name she burst into tears and said, 'Sister, that man was my father.' (He had died 12 months previously.) She said she was unworthy to hear the story while sitting, and knelt on the floor. I knelt beside her. With both of us weeping, we asked God's forgiveness on behalf of the family—she for the damage done by the error and I for any bondage of resentment or unforgiveness that may be deep within my heart.

"God's timing is so perfect. It's been many years now since the healing experience. In my ministry of praying for healing I am deeply conscious of blockages to the healing power of Jesus. I believe some of the greatest of these are: involvement with the occult, resentment and unforgiveness, judgements against others, how we perceived our parents acted toward us, generational sin and hurts received in the womb."

Healing Reflections

* Capture the feelings of your most significant reconciliation with another person.

* What brought about this reconciliation?

* Reflect upon the Lord's forgiveness of you.

* Do you have a healed relationship with yourself?

* In what areas do you still hold something against yourself?

Lord, Have Mercy

I asked the Lord for justice, then I remembered myself, and asked for mercy.

(Author unknown)

All my life I've been saying the *Kyrie Eleison* at Mass. Finally one day it dawned on me, many years after I was ordained into the priesthood, "Lord, have mercy!" I never heard it so deeply before. We are like sponges floating on an ocean of mercy, crying "Mercy." All we need is the capacity to receive, like the sponge. When a sponge has a capacity to receive, water rushes in and the sponge is filled. As we forgive, and receive His forgiveness, then we can soak up the mercy. Mercy means love and forgiveness in action. Psalm 51:1 says, "Have mercy on me, O God, in Your goodness..." The Lord extends His arms to us and says, "Receive my forgiveness, my pardon, my mercy." As you open your heart and say, "Lord, I receive," the dry sponge that has been floating on an ocean of mercy begins to soak up all that waiting grace.

The Lord then holds you up tenderly to His Father, covered in His precious blood, and says, "Mercy." The accuser, the devil, interrupts angrily and asks, "But what about this...and this...and this?" The Father ignores the accuser, looks down at you and sees someone clean and free and whole, washed in the blood of His Son." His heart overflows with joy as He says, "Come, beloved of my Son." There is no time with God. Because He lives in the eternal now He sees us in glory already, and is so happy with our presence.

Kyrie, eleison...Lord have mercy

Christe, eleison...Christ have mercy

Kyrie, eleison...Lord have mercy

Throughout our Christian history the Lord has revealed His constant love and enduring mercy. That mercy is not only the greatest attribute of God, but is His very Nature. As we read in 1John 4:16, "God is love." In 1931 in Poland, the Lord appeared in a vision to Sister M. Faustina Kowalska of the Congregation of the Sisters of Our Lady of Mercy. He asked her to paint a picture of Him signed: "Jesus, I trust in You," and spoke of people coming to Him as a fountain of mercy. "I am Mercy itself," He told her (Diary, 1775). In a subsequent Novena to the Divine Mercy He asked for the following:

Day 1. Bring to Me all mankind, especially all sinners, and immerse them in the ocean of My mercy.

Day 2. Bring to Me the souls of priests and religious and immerse them in My unfathomable mercy.

Day 3. Bring to Me all devout and faithful souls and immerse them in the ocean of My mercy.

Day 4. Bring to Me those who do not believe in Me and those who do not yet know Me...[and] immerse them in the ocean of My mercy.

Day 5. Bring to Me the souls of those who have separated themselves from your Church and immerse them in the ocean of My mercy.

Day 6. Bring to Me the meek and humble souls and the souls of little children, and immerse them in My mercy.

Day 7. Bring to Me the souls who especially venerate

and glorify My mercy, and immerse them in My mercy.

Day 8. Bring to Me the souls who are detained in purgatory and immerse them in the abyss of My mercy.

Day 9. Bring to Me the souls who have become lukewarm and immerse them in the abyss of My mercy. [1]

Dimensions of Mercy

Three Hebrew words that reveal dimensions of mercy are *rahoum, hanoum* and *hesed. Rahoum* suggests motherly compassion: "Can a mother forget her infant, be without tenderness *(rahoum)* for the child of her womb?" (Is 49:15). *Hanoum* suggests sovereign mercy: "O Lord, have pity on me; heal me, though I have sinned against you" (Ps41:5). *Hesed* is the word that the theologians use as grace. It means loving-kindness, covenant mercy. The Jews had a wonderful understanding of God's mercy. Because He had made a covenant with them, they understood His faithfulness. No matter what they did, he would always forgive them: " 'Though the mountains leave their place and the hills be shaken, my love *(hesed)* shall never leave you, nor my covenant of peace be shaken,' says the Lord, who has mercy on you" (Is 54:10).

One circumstance that qualifies us for mercy is extreme need. We might say that love and misery give birth to mercy. In the world today there is a desperate need for mercy. We live in a generation of despair and hopelessness.

The Church is a gathering of sinners appealing to God's mercy, and a model of mercy for the world. Christians are called to heal society, to be healers, to be open and tenderhearted toward others. They are called to extend mercy, to themselves and to the world.

The Lord tells us in *I am Your Jesus of Mercy:*

"Mercy is the divine power of my love, which flows out onto whom ever seeks it. One of the many gifts as you receive My Holy Spirit is that of mercy. When you allow My Divine Love to flow from you, out to someone who is in need, that is My mercy flowing out from Me. When you, or any of My children, have mercy on someone, it is equivalent to Me having mercy on that same person..because of My Spirit, which dwells in you. Mercy is a missing link in loving. You cannot love without being able to have mercy. You cannot have mercy if you do not love! I know this seems very much for you, but you must know the truth. My people ask for My mercy, but they will not give My mercy, because they select not to love, or they select who they desire to love. God does not select...neither should His people."[2]

Works of Mercy

In our childhood catechism we were taught the seven corporal and seven spiritual works of mercy:
Corporal: feed the hungry, give drink to the thirsty, clothe the naked, shelter the homeless, visit the sick, ransom the captive and bury the dead.
Spiritual: instruct the ignorant, counsel the doubtful, admonish sinners, bear wrongs patiently, forgive offenses willingly, comfort the afflicted, pray for the living and the dead.

Model of Mercy

The most prominent model of mercy in the Catholic Church today is Mother Teresa of Calcutta. She challenges each of us to examine our lives in light of the Lord's call for a merciful Church.

Through a psychological experiment in a college with a video observing Mother Teresa at work, insight was gained about the healing power of observing "mercy in action." In the experiment the subjects submitted to a saliva test that indexed the immune response. The participants watched a 60 minute video of the work of Mother Teresa. After the video, 50% indicated a positive response and 50% were negative about the video. Yet all the participants, regardless of how they graded their response to the video, showed on the saliva test a rise in their immune system. It was concluded that in the face of goodness and truth the spirit, mind and body is influenced toward greater health.

Survey Responses

We asked the survey respondents the question, "What is your most profound experience of receiving God's mercy in your daily life?" Some of those responses include:

* I returned to the sacraments after an absence of 17 years. (Fran Rinaldi)

* After communion at an outdoor Mass, I was convicted of all my sins. I was driven across the field away from the congregation to fall on my face in the dirt, and there to be forgiven. (John Heilman)

* I was spared from bitterness, hatred and rash decisions during my husband's midlife crisis. (Traudel W.)

* My whole life is an experience of God's mercy, especially when He healed me of shame and guilt. (Amy F.)

* I was healed of drug addiction, fornication and back pain. (Rodger S.)

* He led my strayed children back into His arms. (Ruth)

* He didn't give up on me. I said "No" to some of His requests, and He patiently keeps after me. (Jerry Weibel)

* He called off my wedding. (Carolyn)

* He showed me He loved me as I am, and hadn't made a mistake in creating me a female, and short. (Christine Stewart)

* I received Jesus as my Lord and Savior after being an agnostic for 30 years. (Peggy Hurtado)

* I was forgiven for my 11-month-old daughter's death. (Edna R.)

* My confession to a priest who accepted me as a worthwhile person, even though I felt like a dung heap. Jesus hugged this little dung heap through the priest during confession. (Joyce C.)

* During my severe struggle with suicidal depression He didn't abandon me to the power of death; He helped me find Him. (Frida M.)

* Someone forgave me when I mistreated him. (Bruce Lizana)

* He shows me that even though I'm a tiny spec in this creation, I shine like a diamond under His gaze. (Frances Young)

* My reception into the Catholic Church 35 years ago at age 23. (Pat Howarth)

* I often experience His mercy when I see street people and panhandlers. I realize how generous and merciful God has always been with me, especially when I was so self-destructive. (Joe Miller)

Mercy in the Womb

"When mother was carrying me in her womb, several physicians recommended that she have an abortion. She refused to listen. Jesus reminded me of that in tough times. I was working in intensive care, taking care of very sick babies that were dying left and right. I felt like a failure and said, "Jesus, why do I feel like I have to fail?" He took me back to the time I was in the womb and said, "It is I who have called you into being. It is I who formed you in your mother's womb. I chose your parents as the best possible parents for you. What I make is perfect. You are loved; you are mine; you are not a failure." Jesus did a deep healing, from the time in the womb to the present. It was a powerful experience of God's mercy in my life."

Healing Reflections

* Take a moment and think of one time you experienced God's mercy.

* Consider a time when you extended mercy.

* Reflect upon a time when you missed extending mercy.

* Consider a way in which the church can extend mercy.

* Think of a need in the world for mercy.

* Think of one way in which you will make a commitment to be more merciful.

7

Gloria

Glory to God in the highest, and peace to His people on earth. Lord God, heavenly King, almighty God and Father, we worship You, we give You thanks, we praise You for Your glory. Lord Jesus Christ, only Son of the Father, Lord God, Lamb of God, You take away the sin of the world: have mercy on us; You are seated at the right hand of the Father: receive our prayer.

In the Penitential Rite we open our hearts to God's forgiving love. We experience His divine forgiveness, His love and compassion and mercy. In the presence of His extraordinary goodness we lift up our hearts in praise as did the angels at the birth of Jesus. "Suddenly, there was with the angel a multitude of the heavenly host, praising God and saying, 'Glory to God in high heaven, peace on earth to those on whom His favor rests' " (Lk 2:13-14). The Blessed Mother has communicated to visionary Mary Constancio of Slayton, Texas, that we should "...listen to and savor each word in the Gloria, which has great power to open our hearts."

In the *Gloria* (one of the earliest praise songs of the Church) we enter into the praise of Jesus before the Father. His prayer becomes our prayer. Our prayer becomes His prayer. We join the earthly priesthood with the heavenly priesthood and together acknowledge God's perfection, His works, and His benefits.

Becoming Praise Centered

As Catholics we tend to be petition-oriented, which has the unfortunate effect of keeping us as the center of our prayer. In praise, Jesus is the center of our prayer. Praise Him! Praise Him! Praise Him! This is what we are called to do with our whole being. As we become praise-conscious people, praising and thanking the Lord for everything and everyone in our lives, we are, in effect, surrendering to Him. We are forgetting about ourselves and concentrating on Him. "Let everything that has breath praise the Lord" (Ps 150:6).

Something happens deep inside when we forget ourselves, direct our attention toward God and pour our hearts into worshiping and praising our creator. We give up the right to understand difficult circumstances and simply surrender them to the Lord in trust. We say, "I don't understand everything that is happening in my life, but I believe in Your love and I trust Your goodness."

What marvelous works the Lord can do in us, for us and through us as we center on His goodness and love. When we praise we are acknowledging the Lord as creator and His continuing, active involvement in our lives. He is the potter, we are the clay (Jer 17:7). As we make this sacrifice of praise in all circumstances, we will become more open to healing of body, mind and spirit.

Jack of Portland, Oregon, shares about a friend's healing that came as he began to praise: "A friend in alcoholics anonymous had open, ulcerated legs that he nearly lost. One night he got on his knees beside the bed in terrible agony and began to thank and praise God for his legs, just as they were. He continued to do so, and his legs gradually began to heal. That happened in 1977. He continues to praise God daily for everything—the good and the difficult."

Praise is healing. In praise we are ministering to the Lord. He says, "Give, and it shall be given to you. Good measure pressed down, shaken together, running over, will they pour into the fold of your garment. For the measure you measure with will be measured back to you" (Lk6:38). In giving praise we receive healing.

Praise is Hard Work

Praise is powerful, but it's hard work. Don't be dismayed if you find it a struggle. Father Chris Aridas says, "It is precisely in the working that the Spirit comes, thereby leading us to true worship (that is, praise that draws its power more from God's promise than from our own feelings and efforts)." [1] "...let us continually offer God a sacrifice of praise, that is, the fruit of lips which acknowledge His name" (Heb13:15).

Attitude of Gratitude

We begin with an "attitude of gratitude," which awakens us to God's love and moves us toward healing. Father Richard Bain of San Francisco, California suggests that we need to give thanks to God informally, like a three year old, who might say, "This is the fire engine you gave me! You gave it to me!" Not formally, but "You did this!" Tell God what He did. Try entering into the mind of that excited child, thanking "Abba, Daddy," for His blessings.

Thank Him for that love that enables you to work, talk, breathe and enjoy life. Thank Him in every circumstance, even when the washing machine breaks down and the children don't come home on time. As we thank Him in the trials of the moment our hearts are opened to the action of the Holy Spirit. Thank Him for your family—not only the godly ancestors who paved the way and made it easier for you to know Him, but also the black sheep who made trouble for the family. Thank Him for the gift of father, mother, sisters and brothers, uncles and aunts, cousins, grandmothers, grandfathers, spouse, children, and grandchildren. Thank Him for relatives who supported, encouraged and cared for you along the way, and those who didn't.

Thank Him for friends, co-workers and associates who helped and encouraged you and those who brought trials. Thank Him for doctors and nurses who performed their duties with compassion and concern and those who didn't. Thank Him for the Roman Catholic Church. Thank Him for all the unnamed people in society who have affected your life in a positive and negative way. Then begin to move from grateful acknowledgment of past mercies to praising Him for His glorious acts in the universe.

> *For You alone are the Holy One, You alone are the Lord, You alone are the Most High, Jesus Christ, with the Holy Spirit, in the glory of God the Father. Amen.*

Healing Reflections

* Reflect upon your highest experience of praise.

* How was that moment healing for you?

8

Oration
"Let us pray."

The first part of the Mass prepares us to hear the word of God. We have been called into His presence, our distractions are gone, and we are asked to join our hearts and minds in prayer. When the priest says, "Let us pray," he is inviting the community to enter into the opening prayer of the Mass, the *Oration.* As the priest prays with arms extended, he gathers or "collects" the prayers and needs of the congregation and presents them to the Lord. He vocalizes for us our needs in a prayer to the Father, through the Son, in the power of the Holy Spirit. It might be something like the following prayer from the 31st Sunday of Ordinary Time:

> *God of power and mercy, only with Your help*
> *can we offer You fitting service and praise. May we*
> *live the faith we profess and trust Your promise of*
> *eternal life.*

When the priest says, "Let us pray," he is saying, "Let us share today the overflow of our prayer life, collecting and presenting our prayers to God our Father." There is healing power in community prayer during Mass, especially when the people have also been praying during the week. If they have been in daily prayer, then the benefits will overflow into the Mass. They will come with something to give. Pope Pius XII said that liturgical prayer nourishes private prayer and private prayer nourishes liturgical prayer. Let's ask for the grace to be faithful in both. [1]

The vitality of a church is dependent to a great extent upon the prayer life of its members. Bishop Fulton Sheen said that the Church could be renewed if everyone spent twenty minutes a day in mental prayer, which includes scripture reading and meditation time. God is calling His people to become people of prayer, not only during Mass, but as a way of life. Dr. Paul Yonggi Cho, the pastor of Yoido Full Gospel Church in Seoul, Korea with a membership of over 600,000 people, has said that the secret of his church's success is twofold. First, the deep commitment to prayer, with continuous intercession at the church's "prayer mountain" where 3,000 are daily in prayer and fasting; and second, the participation of members in small cell groups in weekly home meetings, in addition to the large Sunday worship services. Some of our Catholic parishes that have adopted the small home prayer and share group approach, have reported renewed life in their parishes. One in particular is St. Boniface Church in Pembroke Pines, Florida. Like Dr. Cho's church, this Southern Florida Catholic parish is continually in prayer.

Another pastor, Father Robert Bedard of St. Mary's Church in Ottawa, Ontario, Canada, learned in prayer that God wanted to renew this parish. Pastor and parishioners waited on the Lord in prayer for two years before they saw God do something. Then the pastor began getting reports that people, mostly men, were crying during the Sunday liturgy. Crowds and collections began to increase. Then God placed an anointing on the building. People began to speak about the "touch of God" upon the building, saying "Something is special about this place." Then the Lord began giving a variety of ministries to people, indicating that He would give the signal and provide the power to send them forth. It all began with prayer.

Three Forms of Prayer

There are three legs to a prayer life. The first leg of

the tripod is community prayer, such as Mass or a prayer meeting. The second leg is small group prayer. The third leg is private prayer. People must be challenged to deep personal prayer.

There is a story of a woman with a retarded eighteen-year-old son and a husband who was jealous of the son. One day the woman cried out to the Lord because of the overwhelming problems at home. She began to get a sense that the Lord was calling her to spend quiet time with Him each day. As she responded, over the course of a few weeks she began seeing changes in her family. Finally the whole situation was healed.

You, the reader, should be the intercessor in your home. You may be the only channel through which God's healing power can flow through your family. Daily prayer for family members can work miracles.

A story is told of an atheist, Howard Storm, who considered religion to be a fantasy until he was in a crisis during a business trip to northern Europe. He became ill and needed immediate surgery, but before it could be performed he found himself in an out-of-body experience. At first he found himself in a heavy fog with aggressive people pushing and shoving him around. Finally he fell to the ground and heard his own voice saying, "Pray to God." He began saying the Twenty-third Psalm. As he struggled to recall prayers the creatures around him went into a frenzy. Storm began, "Our Father, who art in heaven..." Then he found himself alone, and singing the children's song, "Jesus loves me..." Into the darkness he then screamed, "Jesus, please save me!" Then he saw a tiny speck of light, which became bigger and bigger." He began to cry, and began feeling things he had never felt. He was surrounded by light and love. Then he was told to go back. Today when he talks in churches around northern Kentucky about his healing and conversion, he tells people that he is alive today because of the intercessory prayers of Notre Dame Sister Mary Dolores and several friends at St. Mary's Church in Alexandria, Kentucky. He did not know about their petitions, however, until he returned to the United States and began telling his story. 2

I have never met a dying person who complained that too much time in life was spent in prayer. Most people on their deathbeds lament the lack of time in prayer. People of prayer will go to Mass and give. So we want to become people of prayer, setting aside a minimum of 15-30 minutes a day for prayer. The Blessed Virgin Mary is asking people in Medjugorje, Yugoslavia, to spend four hours a day in prayer.

Daily Holy Hour

On my "Healing Power of Holy Orders" retreats I challenge the priests to spend a daily holy hour. Bishop Fulton Sheen made a promise on the day of his ordination that he would spend a continuous holy hour every day in the presence of our Lord in the Blessed Sacrament. He kept that promise throughout his life and encouraged other priests to do likewise. Perhaps no other bishop in our modern time has had such a powerful influence on American Catholics. I believe his power flowed from his daily prayer life.

As a priest I feel the obligation to spend at least one hour in prayer daily with the Eucharistic Lord, and have kept this commitment from the day I first entered the seminary. In fact, I have extended the time to three hours a day in recent years. I could not accomplish the work of priest retreats to which the Lord has called me without faithfulness to time with the Lord before the Blessed Sacrament. Many priests have said this type of retreat is the best they have ever made. We have a daily holy hour in the busy retreat schedule.

Becoming People of Prayer

My experience over the years as a priest has proven to me that people of prayer are basically happier people and are more able to cope with the "hard knocks" of life than those who do not pray. As Catholics we need to realize the very serious obligation to become people of prayer. We have been blessed immeasurably in our faith with a loving heavenly Father, Jesus as Lord, the power of the Holy Spirit, the sacraments, scripture, the Blessed Mother, our Church community. Let us respond with a serious prayer life to these gifts of God. As Jesus said to the Samaritan woman, "If only you recognized God's gift..." (Jn 4:10).

Survey Responses

In the survey we asked the respondents if they prayed before the Blessed Sacrament. A few comments from the 77 who responded "Yes" are recorded below:

* Once I went into church and just poured out all kinds of troubles and pains. Then I heard the words, "But can you dance before me?" Since I was the only one in church, I did, and it was wonderful. (Eileen Smith)

* I talk to Jesus, talk to my Heavenly Father, talk to the Holy Spirit, talk to the Blessed Mother. It's all one-on-one time, and very special. (Jim Franke)

* Sometimes after feeding the street people and hardly anyone is in church, I will visit and talk with the Lord. It's so peaceful. Sometimes a soft breeze will blow and a ray of sun will shine down on me. On some occasions I feel electricity and warmth in my hands. (Adrienne Winchester)

* Spending time before the Blessed Sacrament makes me more daring to minister to strangers and some acquaintances. (Carmen Sale)

* It's the easiest place to center myself. I don't have a special story but I always leave the church whistling. (Ming O'Neill)

* Sometimes during my night adoration time I sing to Jesus. Other times I dance for Him. Most of the time I just cry from happiness. (Frida Molina)

* Every time I feel worried too much I pray before the Blessed Sacrament. I gain strength and feel peaceful. Once I even heard Jesus speak. He said to me, "Do you trust me?" (Ann Nham)

* I lose track of time and get carried away conversing with the Lord. (Virginia Zandueta)

* Because of my private prayer time before the Blessed Sacrament I've grown more and more aware of God's presence in every moment, every day, every circumstance. (Joe Miller)

* Once I spent all night in the chapel. I had been misunderstood and felt very hurt. I was healed. The truth came to light, and it was great! (Leroy Behnke)

Grant this through our Lord Jesus Christ,
Your Son, who lives and reigns with You and the
Holy Spirit, one God, for ever and ever. Amen.

Healing Reflections

* Reflect upon the strengths and weaknesses of your prayer life.

* Are the three legs of your prayer life in place?

PART III

LITURGY OF THE WORD

Scripture Readings

...let the 'word of the Lord run and be glorified'
(2 Thes3:1) and let the treasure of revelation
entrusted to the Church increasingly fill the
hearts of men. Just as the life of the Church grows
through persistent participation in the
Eucharistic mystery, so we may hope for a new
surge of spiritual vitality from intensified
veneration for God's word, which 'lasts forever'
(Is40:8; cf. 1Pet1:23-25). [1]

The gospel sequence of the Mass begins with the priest saying, "Almighty God, cleanse my heart and my lips that I may worthily proclaim Your gospel." He invokes God's healing touch upon his heart and on his lips. The congregation responds by repeating this healing gesture as they, too, ask that the words of the gospel be burned into their minds, upon their lips, into their hearts, into their consciousness, that they, with the celebrant, may act on the word. "Act on this word. If all you do is listen to it, you are deceiving yourselves" (Jas1:22).

By this time we should be in tune to hear the word of the Lord in the Liturgy of the Word. According to Father Richard Bain of San Francisco, California, "When the dynamic is properly set up during the Introductory Rites, our minds will be pulled from daydreaming to hear the word of the Lord." Everyone is together. All are ready to listen, receptive and open to hear and be moved by the word of God. All introductory parts contribute to a readiness to hear the word of the Lord. We have adored and praised God, expressed sorrow for sins and asked for mercy.

If we prayerfully read the scriptures ahead of time we will have already predigested them. We will be open to the Lord so that when the lector proclaims the word we will hear it in our hearts. Our ears are so open, our hearts are so ready, that its full effect is produced. When the lector finishes the readings and says, "This is the word of the Lord," we can truly say, "Yes, we have heard! Yes, that's for me. Thank you, Lord, I needed that!"

When I was a pastor in Prairie View, Texas we would have a scripture study Thursday mornings, based on the readings of the Sunday Mass. We would read them and have a time for personal reflection and sharing. This is an excellent idea for those people wanting to begin small sharing groups. I encourage priests to share the readings with a group of lay people to get ideas for the Sunday homilies. By listening to the responses of lay people the priests can speak at a meaningful level. I deeply enjoyed my Thursday sharings and found that lay people had valuable insights stemming from years of Christian living in their vocations as single adults, marriage partners and parents. I would use the people's insights in my Sunday homily and was thus able to be on their wavelength.

Scripture is God Breathed

"All scripture is inspired of God..." (2 Tim3:16). The *Documents of Vatican II* state, "Those divinely revealed realities which are contained and presented in sacred scripture have been committed to writing under the inspiration of the Holy Spirit." [2]

As the Liturgy of the Word begins, ask the Holy Spirit to speak through the scripture verses with a word of instruction, insight, understanding, healing. Be open to receive that intimate word. Open yourself to the work the Holy Spirit wants to accomplish that day.

I remember reading a book of private revelations to a priest, in which the Lord Jesus said: "People do not listen. They did not listen back in my age and they still do not listen now. They hear what they want to hear. They select their words over mine." [3]

The Holy Spirit often leads people to pray for others with scripture. He prompts some to memorize verses. He guides all of us to continually renew our minds, replacing our thoughts by thoughts expressed in the word of God.

Ramona's Story

Ramona was 37 when she made a commitment to Jesus and asked Him to be Lord of her life. Five years later she became romantically involved with a non-practicing Catholic and walked away from God. As you read her story, ponder the variety of ways, especially through scripture, that the Lord used to bring her back.

"After living for two years with a man named Sam, who was not my husband, our relationship ended in a very ugly way. I was filled with anger, bitterness, resentment and unforgiveness. I was especially angry because he owed me $5,000, and I hired a lawyer to get it back. After a healing Mass at my church a friend who was praying for me said the word 'forgive.' I couldn't stop crying because I was sure I could never forgive him. Later when I was wondering if I had done the right thing in leaving the relationship, I overheard one sentence in a nearby conversation: 'Anything that takes you away from Jesus becomes an idol.' I realized that I had replaced Jesus with Sam, and had committed idolatry.

"During a weekend conference in San Francisco with Father Robert DeGrandis and his sister Dorothea, I received more healing. During Dorothea's meditation on emotionally 'cutting the cords' to the people we are bound to, I let go of Sam and cried my heart out. At that moment I also felt a 'popping' in my right abdomen. I had been having gall bladder symptoms and my doctor suggested later, when I mentioned it to him, that I might have passed a gallstone at that moment. The healing was further verified when Father DeGrandis spoke of the healing of stomachs. Later that day I had an appetite for the first time in a month. Father DeGrandis took us through a forgiveness prayer that same day and asked us to commit to saying it for a month. I started on the program.

"A week later during the Southern California Renewal Convention in Anaheim, California, I was in the arena listening to John Michael Talbot telling the story of the wedding at Cana, where Mary told the servants to 'Do what He tells you,' when he changed the water to wine. In my spirit I knew that was God telling me to let go of the $5,000 debt. This was the one cord connecting me to Sam.

"On my return flight home from the conference I was reading about the 'unjust steward' and saw myself in the parable. I was emotionally choking Sam and saying 'pay back what you owe me.' I decided to let go of the debt. I wrote a letter to him and told him that I was forgiving the debt. I forgave him for hurting me and asked forgiveness for hurting him. I also contacted my lawyer to cancel impending legal action. A few days later I spent 3-1/2 hours with Sam. We walked and talked and forgave each other.

"I don't know if I will ever see him again, because I have truly let him go. I praise Jesus for pulling me out of sin and darkness and for taking the prodigal daughter back. My heart is still in the process of healing the hurt, but the bitterness, resentment, unforgiveness and anger are gone."

Using Scripture in Active Imagination

Using scripture in active imagination is powerful, as in the example of Ramona's experience of cutting of the cords, based on John 11:44, when Jesus said, "...Unbind him, and let him go." In my sister Dorothea's book, *The Healing Jesus in Scripture*, she recommends the following: "In your mind's eye see that person standing opposite you, and see if there is a

cord running from your forehead to his forehead...
from your head to his head...trying to make you think
the way he thinks or putting your ideas into his head.
See if there is a cord from your mouth to his mouth,
cord of criticism, words of put-down...from your heart
to his heart...from your hands to their hands. Perhaps
there were things you wanted to do and they never
allowed you to do them, or things they wanted to do
and you never allowed them to do. Perhaps this person
is trying to manipulate or control you. Are there cords
from your sexual organs to theirs? Perhaps someone
has you in bondage sexually. Are there cords from your
feet to their feet, not allowing you to go places you
wanted to go? If there is someone who has smothered
you, just see the cords wrapped around your neck, from
your neck to his neck.

"Now see Jesus come into the picture, and in His
hand He has the most beautiful sword you have ever
seen. It is a golden sword, long and very sharp. It is the
Word of God. It can cut through soul and spirit. Now
Jesus says to you, 'Will you give Me permission to cut
these cords? I would not cut these cords if it weren't for
a higher purpose, for a greater relationship, a
relationship built on love and not need'...Silently
within you say, 'Yes, Jesus, I give You permission to cut
those cords and set me free and set them free.'

"After He cuts the cords He walks over to the other
person, puts His arms around him and leads him out of
the room. He might say to the person, 'You are in my
care. I will lead you in a path that is just right for you.'
Then He comes back into the room and with His arms
around you, says, 'I am sufficient to meet all your
needs. The world can no longer control you. I will
renew your mind. Look to Me. Let Me teach you My
truth and light. I want you to be that free, loving
person I created you to be.' Affirm your freedom by
saying, 'Thank You, Lord, for setting them free and
setting me free.' " [4] There is healing power in the word
of God.

Scripture tells us, "For neither herb nor poultice
cured them, but it was thy word, O Lord, which heals
all men" (Wis16:12, JB). Shirley Filadelfia of San Juan

Capistrano, California, has a powerful story about the healing power of the word of God. The thrombo phlebitis in her legs was so advanced that the doctor recommended hospitalization and the use of a blood thinner. As you read her story, ask the Holy Spirit to penetrate your spirit with His word so deeply, that in a crisis you will respond in a similar way.

Shirley's Story

"One night during my stay at Martin Luther Hospital in Southern California I woke up out of a sound sleep. I couldn't breathe, and felt like there was a heavy rock in my chest. I tried to take a breath but nothing happened; no air would go into my lungs. I was filled with fear. In the dark room I buzzed the nurse.

"As she entered the room and turned on the light my eyes were drawn to the picture of Jesus on the opposite wall. The instant my eyes lit on the picture I felt His presence. I knew I was dying, but all fear was gone.

"The nurse signalled code blue and everyone came running. When the charge nurse exchanged glances with the nurse at my bedside, she just shook her head. Then the charge nurse (who was not a Christian) recognized me. We had known each other for some time, and were friends. She ran over and scooped me up in her arms. As she did this my whole left side went numb. When I saw the tears streaming down her face, I deeply needed to respond to them, but I couldn't breathe.

"And yet somehow the words came out: 'The Lord is my Shepherd; I shall not want...' (Ps 23). As I spoke the word of God, air entered my lungs. They call it the Living Word. The word of God is the breath of life to me. I learned later that a blood clot had traveled from my leg to my heart valve, and was visible on the monitor. Father Bruce and Margaret arrived to pray for me. After I received the sacrament of the sick the blood clot was no longer visible on the monitor. Later tests revealed a large mass in my abdomen that required surgery. The clots had come from that area.

I was healed in four ways: (1) seeing the face of Jesus I was emotionally healed from panic; (2) in the spoken Word He gave physical healing of air in my lungs; (3) in the sacramental anointing the blood clot disappeared; (4) through the surgeon's skill the root cause was removed."

"...to my words be attentive, to my sayings incline your ear; Let them not slip out of your sight, keep them within your heart; For they are life to those who find them, to a man's whole being they are health" (Pro4:20-22).

Untapped Riches

A friend in Texas was very, very poor for many years. An oil company came and discovered oil on her property in 1980. My friend was soon very, very rich. Actually, she was rich all along, but she didn't know it. Her treasure was in the ground under her feet! The same is true with us. We have a spiritual heritage with many untapped riches. The Kingdom of God is within! As we surrender our lives to Christ, all that He is and all that He has is ours. This is our inheritance as sons and daughters of the King of Kings, but we continue to act as if we are poor, poor, poor. We must receive our inheritance.

We gain access to our inheritance through prayerful study of the word of God under the guidance of the Holy Spirit. It is through a deep, intimate relationship with the Holy Spirit that we will begin to enter into our inheritance.

Jesus Teaches About Life

When I was in the seminary, I was sent to summer camp each year. One evening when I was sitting on the stairs of a boathouse by the river on lifeguard duty I flipped open my New Testament to John 10:10, "...I came that they might have life, and have it to the full." It was just like a lightning bolt from heaven. The thought came to me, "Jesus wants me to be happy!" That changed my whole attitude toward religion. From that time on I believed in my heart that religion is meant to be uplifting and joyful.

Linda Schubert from Sunnyvale, California, shares about her life-changing scripture in the following story: "After I was baptized in the Holy Spirit, following the death of my step-son, Randy, the Lord impressed on me the verse "I have set before you life and death...choose life..." (Deut30:19). In the years to come I went through some desperate trials, times I felt so low I would literally be flat on the floor in deep depression. I remember one day in particular when I was in terrible despair. I heard the Lord whisper, "Linda, choose life." Gritting my teeth with no energy and no faith, I said flatly, "I choose life." It was only a mental assent, but in two or three minutes I felt life and strength beginning to rise up inside. Within a half hour I was out of my depression and functioning normally."

As Father Edmund "Ted" Shipp of San Francisco, California, says, "In the gospels, Jesus teaches what it means to have 'life.' He meets people in their needs and wants and, if they are open, He touches them and heals them. Some were blocked by their sins and needed to be freed from them. A man who was paralyzed needed a greater healing than the physical. The point of the readings is to inspire us to want to be open to let Jesus act in and through us in the same way, that we, too, may have a new surge of spiritual, emotional and physical vitality."

We have untapped riches! "Come. You have my Father's blessing. Inherit the kingdom prepared for you from the creation of the world" (Mt25:34).

His Words are Trustworthy

For three nights a young Christian woman had been anxiously studying for nursing school exams at Charity Hospital in New Orleans, Louisiana. As she opened her Bible looking for words of encouragement, the words that spoke to her were: "Trust in the Lord with all your heart; on your own intelligence rely not" (Pro3:5). During her exams she repeated that verse over and over, and passed with an "A".

The question of trust is important to all. We all come to a point where we have to ask ourselves: "Can I trust God with my life, which is so precious to me? How much can I trust Him?" We have all been hurt in our lives. Some of us have made vows, in the midst of pain, never to trust, never to love, never to open up again. It hurts too much when we are open and vulnerable and are taken advantage of in that vulnerability.

The Lord wants us to know that He is a trustworthy friend. At some point in our lives everyone else will let us down, but He will never let us down. 2 Samuel 7:28 says, "You are God, and your words are truth..." Psalm 111:7 tells us, "The works of His hands are faithful and just; sure are all His precepts."

Three internationally known evangelists—Oral Roberts, Kenneth Hagin and Dr. Paul Yonggi Cho—were dying as teenagers. In each case someone came to them and said, "Look at the word of God. It says that God heals. Ask and you will receive." Each believed in the word of God, trusted that He was who He said He was, trusted that He would do what He promised. Each was healed. (Dr. Cho was not even a Christian at the time.)

All trust involves some risk, a venturing into an uncertain realm, a leap of faith. I pray for each of us that we will continue to grow in faith, grow in trust, and keep our eyes on Jesus. "...No one who believes in Him will be put to shame" (Rom10:11).

When the Word Takes Root

"How I love your law, O Lord! It is my meditation all the day" (Ps119:97). Deuteronomy 11:18 states, "...take these words of mine into your heart and soul. Bind them at your wrist as a sign, and let them be a pendant on your forehead." Mary, in Luke 2:51, speaks of "treasuring all these things in our hearts." The Blessed mother encourages us, through the visionaries in Medjugorje, Yugoslavia, to take one verse a month and meditate on it over and over. I shared with you the one verse that changed my life. A nun spent five months on just the verse, "God is love" (1 Jn4:16). Some people in the healing ministry maintain that when a scripture strikes you, if you keep repeating it over and over it takes root and brings healing.

A guard at a state prison in the South started a Bible study for prisoners during the summer. Many signed up to get out of the hot sun on the farm. The method used by the teacher was to have the men memorize the book of Romans! As they started to memorize the scripture daily, the Holy Spirit started to work in their spirits. They came to a point where they had to accept either what they were memorizing or go back to the farm. Most went back to the vegetables rather than continue ingesting the word that they could not believe. Those who stayed were converted. One of them, when questioned by me about his sentence, said: "I am serving 35 years for murder but I have never been happier in my life." When we take the word of God into our spirits, the Holy Spirit will quicken it so that it will affect us profoundly. "God's word is living and effective, sharper than any two-edged sword. It penetrates and divides soul and spirit, joints and marrow; it judges the reflections and thoughts of the heart" (Heb4:12).

A group from Father Rick Thomas' community in El Paso went into the men's prison to minister to the inmates. They brought along a double edged sword—this passage of scripture: "...at Jesus' name every knee must bend in the heaven, on the earth and under the earth, and every tongue proclaim to the glory of God the Father: JESUS CHRIST IS LORD" (Phil2:10-11). "'The first visit was unspeakable,' writes Rick Thomas. 'The stench of urine filled the place. Prisoners were yelling, jeering at us, cursing. Even with the loud speakers we had brought, our voices could not be heard in the uproar.' Confident that the Lord could do the impossible, the musicians that had come with us began to play a song based on Philippians 10:11: Jesus is His name. 'Every knee shall bow, every tongue confess that Jesus Christ is Lord.' After an hour-and-a-half these words came true. A number of inmates were on their knees weeping. Several sank to the hard cement floor of the prison...prisoners began to flock to us, asking us to pray over them...many felt a deep experience of the Lord." [5] " 'Is not my word like fire,' says the Lord, 'like a hammer shattering rocks?' " (Jer 23:29).

Repetition of scripture can lead to right theology. A newspaper article told the story of a man named Ernie Hollands who lives near my mother's home in Massachusetts. He was in and out of jail from age 16 to 40. When he was due to appear before the parole board, it occurred to him that he might impress authorities if he, as others he had heard about, would turn to the Lord. He reported: "I went through the Bible five times, reading 15-20 chapters a day. Then I realized something was happening to me on the inside. I didn't hate anymore, I didn't argue any more. I was making friends. One night in my jail cell I saw Jesus. He came in, put His hand on my shoulder and said, 'Ernie Hollands, your slate is wiped clean.' The love and the compassion that flowed from His being was something I'll never forget if I live to be 100. Long into the night I sat on the narrow cot in my cell. Tears flowed freely, mingled with the cleansing flow of the forgiveness of Christ. In that moment there was a transformation. The hardened, habitual criminal became a new born creature in Christ Jesus. Old things were passed away and all things became new. My scoffing at religion stopped. My dirty, filthy mind, my rotten habits, all were cleansed. I was a new person."

That is the Good News we hear in scripture. We hear how impossible it is to rehabilitate criminals, yet we are seeing the transforming power of the word of God.

Repetition can lead to healing. There was a case of a baby born with a damaged brain. The doctor said the child would never be normal. The parents were great believers in the power of the word of God, and taped a cassette with healing verses from scripture, and played it over and over in the crib during waking hours. A month later an examination revealed that the child was completely healed. The brain was totally normal. There is power in the word of God. "The words I spoke to you are Spirit and life" (Jn 6:63). We grow in faith as we hear God's word.

The Deeper Truths of Life

Scripture tells us that, "all who believe will have eternal life in Him" (Jn 3:15). Time in scripture leads us into eternal values. We are led to reflect upon death, judgment, eternity, heaven and hell; where we've come from; where we're going; God's plan for our lives. Time in scripture leads us to lift our eyes above the horizon of our day by day concerns to the very heart of human life. As we study the scriptures, the Holy Spirit will teach us the deeper truths of life.

Rev. Lawrence Jenco spent 19 months as a prisoner in Lebanon, often enduring some appalling deprivations. Some months after his release when he was speaking at a convention of Catholic campus ministers in New Orleans, Father Jenco said that he relied on "three great nourishments" while he was imprisoned—Mass, the Bible and conversation. He knew the Eucharistic prayers by heart, and used ordinary bread for communion hosts.

If you were a prisoner, or were dying, and someone said, "I have God's word here for you," don't you think you would listen? It would be something you would want to take in. Don't wait for a crisis. Begin now to absorb the word of God. One helpful hint is to leave a

Bible on the kitchen table. (Life revolves around the kitchen table.) From time to time ask the Lord to speak to you through a verse. Just as you nibble on food during the day, nibble on scripture during the day. We must be rooted in God's word; the word is intended to inflame our hearts so that we want to respond to the Lord.

The word of the Lord as we hear it and respond to it in our hearts can be healing whenever we attend Mass. The prayers, responses, psalms and suggested songs for the Mass focus upon the scripture readings. It is here that we find the theme that runs through the entirety of Mass. All prayers during the Mass support that theme. Listen for it as you attend your next Mass. God is speaking to His people in a powerful way, calling us to receive His healing love.

This is the word of the Lord.
Thanks be to God.

Healing Reflections

* What is your life-changing scripture verse?

* Consider taking one verse a week and repeat it several times a day. What verse would you start with?

10

Homily

By means of the homily the mysteries of the faith and the guiding principles of the Christian life are expounded from the sacred text... [1]

When I was a pastor in Prairie View, Texas I told the people to come to Mass Sunday expecting to be healed. I would teach them to expect healing; expect to experience God's love; expect Him to move in their lives and meet all their needs. I taught them to expect a miracle.

It was surprising to learn, when they reported back to me about their healing, that so many received healing during the proclamation of the word of God, and the opening up of the word in the homily. In a recent poll, 70% responded that the main source of inspiration was the Sunday homily.

The goal of this section is to: (1) examine the homily from a healing perspective; (2) bring out some points that may help the homilist be an instrument of healing; and (3) help the listener to receive the healing offered.

Healing Perspective

The director of the Theologate for the Laity in Colombo, Sri Lanka, told a news reporter one time that the Catholic Church should give renewed attention to the apostolate of healing, to counter the lure of the sects that offer powerful healing services.

One thing that draws people to those services is the powerful preaching, accompanied by signs and wonders. When the preaching in our churches is accompanied by signs and wonders we don't have enough room to hold the people. People flock to where healing is experienced. "The eleven went forth and preached everywhere. The Lord continued to work with them throughout and confirm the message through the signs which accompanied them" (Mk 16:20).

Healing, and opportunities for healing, build hope in people. Homilies that primarily say what Jesus has done for us will offer healing and hope: He loves us, He died for us, He forgives us; the gift is ours. Homilies that say "We should to do this; we should do that; we should be more humble; we should pray more; we should share with the poor" can sometimes bring more discouragement than healing. The homilist who brings encouragement and hope brings life.

Survey respondent Sylvia McNeill shares this story: "During Mass at St. Thomas Church one night Father Uzral spoke on the power and grace of forgiveness. After Mass I requested prayer for areas of unforgiveness. I cried, and cried that evening. I was told this was a gift of tears."

As we help people realize that God loves them and forgives them—that he created them for a purpose and has a plan to give them a future and a hope (Jer 29:11)—they will grow in trust and faith. Our main purpose is to help them get connected to the God of hope. "...may God, the source of hope, fill you with all joy and peace in believing so that through the power of the Holy Spirit you may have hope in abundance" (Rom15:13).

As the message of the Gospel is unfolded and explained for the congregation there is often a thought, an inspiration or a challenge that will help the listener become more open to the Lord's healing love. Many times during the homily a scripture verse heard earlier becomes a *rhema*, a life-giving word from the Lord. The Lord is speaking throughout the Liturgy of the Word, drawing people into a deeper awareness of His presence and love.

The homily has great potential to open our hearts. As with the disciples on the road to Emmaus, our eyes are opened to see the healing presence of Jesus in scripture. "...two of them that same day were making their way to a village named Emmaus seven miles distant from Jerusalem, discussing as they went all that had happened. In the course of their lively exchange, Jesus approached and began to walk along with them. However, they were restrained from recognizing Him....(then)...Beginning...with Moses and all the prophets, He interpreted for them every passage of scripture which referred to Him...When he had seated Himself with them to eat, He took bread, pronounced the blessing, then broke the bread and began to distribute it to them. With that their eyes were opened and they recognized Him; whereupon He vanished from their sight. They said to one another, 'Were not our hearts burning inside us as He talked to us on the road and explained the scriptures to us?' " (Lk24:13-16, 27, 30-32).

The power that flows through us to others comes from our intimacy with Jesus far more than any skills learned in a course in homiletics. Mother Teresa of Calcutta probably would not pass a seminary test in homiletics. She does everything "wrong." She stands very still and never moves around; she doesn't vary the inflections in her voice; she says the same thing over and over. Yet people weep when she speaks because the Spirit of God pours through her so powerfully. People are convicted and converted while listening to this simple, little, holy woman.

One survey respondent, Amy Falgout, reflected, "We can tell the difference in a Mass that is offered by a priest filled with the Holy Spirit and one who is just there doing his job. One leaves us with a light, holy feeling; the other with a somewhat empty feeling."

The most important thing we can ever teach people is to say "Yes" to the Holy Spirit. After the homily we might ask ourselves (and others) the following: Did it draw people deeper into praise and worship? Did the people feel loved? When deep in their hearts people know they are loved, then their hearts will open to receive the message. The world gives them enough judgment and criticism. People come to church to find love and forgiveness. Priests need to communicate that love in the homily. "We have come to know and to believe in the love God has for us. God is love, and he who abides in love abides in God, and God in him" (1 Jn4:16).

For the Homilist

"Father," commented Amy Falgout again, "the homily is so important. This is what stirs things up. This is what will get people who don't understand into church. A good homily gets a person thinking and examining the things of life."

My father always put great value on the Sunday sermon, and communicated that value to me. Preachers from my boyhood had a great impact on my maturing mind. Since my youth I have been firmly convinced of the power that can be present in the Sunday homily.

Priests and deacons develop their own techniques for preaching. I would like to pass on to them the following guidelines that have proven helpful to me.

1. PRAY FOR AN HOUR SOMETIME BEFORE GIVING THE SUNDAY SERMON. If we put in prayer time, the Holy Spirit will touch both the preacher and the congregation so that sermons will be more effective. As men of faith, we must believe in the value of prayer. A certain country preacher in his first pastorate was considered a very poor preacher. He stumbled and did not articulate well. A group of women in the parish gathered to pray for this bumbling preacher, meeting weekly to hold him up in prayer. Later he went on to become one of the most influential religious leaders in the world. His name is Billy Graham! Get other people to pray for your ministry. I have prayer-partner cards for those people willing to pray for my ministry fifteen minutes a week, or roughly two minutes a day. There

are 50,000 in different languages in circulation now. If only 10% of the people actually do pray, that is 5,000. "...apart from Me you can do nothing" (Jn 15:5b).

2. SPEAK OUT OF PERSONAL EXPERIENCE. Share what the Lord has done in your life and what scripture passages mean to you. People want to know our inner strivings and lights. They are interested in our relationship with the Lord. As Barbara Collins said in the survey, "Father, please share your daily struggles with your people. They suffer the same as you, and need to share in open, honest community for mutual healing." Another respondent, Patsy Gonzales, added, "Many of us compartmentalize our spiritual lives and secular lives. As your heartfelt homilies weave scripture into our daily lives we will be more integrated."

3. USE STORIES AND ILLUSTRATIONS FROM TV AND NEWSPAPERS. Because people are tuned into the media, the use of familiar quotations will catch their attention. One priest uses a *Time* magazine cover as a weekly illustration for his sermon. Another uses excerpts from the Sunday paper in the pulpit.

4. SHARE THE GOOD NEWS OF JESUS CHRIST. Because we live in a depressing world, people need to be uplifted. Only Jesus can give answers for happiness in this nuclear world. Let's give hope to a depressed nation.

Once when an evangelist came to a revival only one young man showed up. He went on and preached as if he had a full church. The young man, Billy Sunday, was converted and went on to become one of this country's greatest preachers.

5. GET LOUD ONCE OR TWICE IN A SERMON. We need to emphasize what we are saying. A preacher once told a Catholic priest, "We preach, you lecture." Enthusiasm is sometimes missing. People need to hear us get excited about the Good News of Jesus Christ.

6. SPEAK ABOUT PRACTICAL SUBJECTS. Sometimes people say we are on a different level and are missing the people's needs. We must make practical and relevant the important themes of the New Testament, such as "Who is Jesus Christ to you?" "Forgiveness," "Faith," "Prayer," "Justice," "Self-Acceptance," and "Love."

7. BE POSITIVE AND INSPIRE. People change by encountering the person of Jesus Christ. Some people complain that they come away depressed because the homilies are negative. We are preaching to set people on fire with the love of Jesus. Once when I was a young priest, a teenage girl asked me why I preach since it is a "waste" of time. That really floored me, but as the years have gone on, I have come to realize that most people are looking for inspiration and affirmation. They hunger for the word of the Lord. I hope she no longer sees it as a waste of time!

8. PROVIDE FOLLOW-UP MATERIAL. I always try to have a pamphlet or a book available so people can continue to absorb the theme of the homily and continue to nourish their minds. We should expect people to read the material given out as they leave church. We are battling for people's minds and need to provide ongoing exposure to Christian literature.

9. ENCOURAGE READING OF DAILY SCRIPTURE. Many Catholics are lured from the Church by an emphasis on scripture by other denominations. We need to show Catholics the value of daily reading and meditating on the word of God.

I pray that these suggestions will prove helpful and increase your skills in preaching.

For the Congregation

The Lord will speak to us and provide help for our circumstances in life. The homily is one of His means of communication. The following are a few practical suggestions for listening to a homily.

1. EXPECT. Before the homily begins, say to the Lord, "I believe you will speak to me through the homily today. The words I hear will penetrate my mind, sink into my heart, produce change and bring healing." Because the Lord is interested in speaking to you, you may even hear things during the homily that the preacher never said. Often people will come up to me after Mass and say, "Father, during the homily I heard you say...and that was just what I needed to hear." A little surprised, I would say, "I don't recall saying that." The Lord lets them hear what is helpful to them at that time in their lives. Many priests have this experience.

Often the Lord will anoint the priest to speak the words He would have him speak, and anoint the people to hear what He wants them to hear. Both are anointed because the church is a sacred place where the anointed word brings healing.

In listening to the homily, ask yourself these questions: "What is God saying at this time? What do I need to hear?" Listening requires a posture of expectancy.

The early Christians lived in the belief that the Lord Jesus was with them; that He was alive; that He was daily revealing Himself to them. Their expectations were fulfilled as the Lord worked healings and miracles in and through them. May we live in the same expectation today as the homilist explains the life-giving words of Jesus!

2. REFLECT. "...Mary treasured all these things and reflected on them them in her heart" (Lk 2:19). When an idea captures your attention during Mass, don't let it get away. Write it down, post it in a visible place and allow the Lord to unfold its meaning in the coming days. The words of scripture are life-giving. When Jesus said, "I have come that they might have life and have it to the full" (Jn 10:10), they were not idle words. Trust that Jesus has come to bring happiness, peace and healing. Trust that He will bring you to new life.

Trust that His word for you will come to pass. "So shall my word be that goes forth from my mouth; it shall not return to me void, but shall do my will, achieving the work for which I sent it" (Is 55:1).

We grow in faith as we deeply reflect upon God's word and allow it to take root and produce change in our hearts.

3. RESPOND. "Act on this word. If all you do is listen to it, you are deceiving yourselves. A man who listens to God's word but does not put it into practice is like a man who looks into a mirror at the face he was born with: he looks at himself, and then goes off and promptly forgets what he looked like. There is, on the other hand, the man who peers into freedom's ideal law and abides by it. He is no forgetful listener, but one who carries out the law in practice. Blessed will this man be in whatever he does" (Jas 1:22-25).

When we come to a knowledge of truth it calls forth a response. I am reminded of a story I heard about a man who became a priest in his early fifties because he came in contact with something that changed his life. While at this writing I can't verify the story, I learned that he was a research scientist at NASA, working with a camera that could gauge and measure on the screen the aura of light around a human body. I believe it is Kirlian photography. NASA's interest was in being able to identify and monitor the aura of the astronauts in orbit, to determine what is happening to them internally. What they found was that dying people have a very thin aura, like blue light, which gets weaker and weaker until the people die. The scientist and an associate were in a hospital apparently behind a two way mirror monitoring the aura of a dying man. As they watched, another man came into the room and filled the room with light, which emanated from his pocket. The man reached into his pocket and did something that caused the camera to be so filled with light that they were unable to see what was happening. They ran into the room only to discover the man giving communion to the dying man. They raced back to the camera and observed that as the dying man received communion his aura began to grow stronger.

The scientist knew, at that point, that there was a higher power; there was someone to be reckoned with, someone for whom he had to live his life. He left his job and became a Catholic priest.

Once we acknowledge something, once we see something deeply, it carries with it a responsibility and an accountability. "When much has been given a man, much will be required of him..." (Lk 12:48).

How are you going to respond to the word you heard in the homily? Perhaps the gospel reading one day was on forgiveness, a major theme of the scriptures, and the Lord reminded you of an area of bitterness in your heart. Would you act upon His word and forgive the one who hurt you?

Acting upon God's word produces healing. He loves us, He speaks to us, and He invites us to open our hearts to the healing He offers. Let's expect Him to speak, reflect upon the words He does speak, and respond to His message of healing for our lives.

Healing Reflections

* What homily in the past month has touched you deeply?

* How did you respond to it?

11

Creed

We believe in one God, the Father, the Almighty, maker of heaven and earth, and of all that is seen and unseen.

We believe in one Lord, Jesus Christ, the only Son of God, eternally begotten of the Father...

We believe in the Holy Spirit, the Lord, the giver of life, who proceeds from the Father and the Son.

We believe in one holy catholic and apostolic Church.

As we stand and say the *Creed*, we stand and make a decision for Christ in our lives. Just as non-Catholic evangelists ask people to make a decision to accept Jesus in an "altar call," we, as Catholics, make our profession of faith during Mass. We are publicly proclaiming that we accept Jesus Christ as Lord.

Some Catholics say, "I was never saved (in the Protestant sense of a deep awareness of Jesus as personal savior) before I went to a non-Catholic church." Catholics are often saved but need to be reminded of this truth. I was saved when I made my first confession at age seven at St. Michael's Church in Lowell, Massachusetts. I knelt down and said, "Father, forgive me because I have sinned." Then when I made my first communion I accepted Jesus into my heart. Many of us were saved as children but, just like our non-Catholic friends, dropped out of fellowship with the Lord and our church community. Catholics especially need to be reminded of their early Christian teachings, beliefs and profession of faith.

When we recite the *Creed* we are exercising the priceless gift of free will. God loves us so much that He endows us with one of the greatest gifts, the gift of free will. You can say "No" to him. I can say "No" to him. All of us are probably still saying "No" to him in certain areas of our lives. But when we are ready to say "Yes," when we are ready to open the door, our loving Father fills us with His love. When we say "Yes, Lord," the Spirit comes and moves in us and through us in a powerful way.

When we recite the *Creed*, we are asking the Father for the grace to consent to have Him possess us and use us.

> *Lord, I ask today for the grace to say 'Yes' to You. Lord, I've sinned, but I repent of my sins. You have forgiven me. I ask today for the grace to forgive myself. I ask You, Lord, to fill me with Your Holy Spirit and fill me with love. Fill me with healing, fill me with peace, fill me with joy. Thank You, Lord, because I believe as I open the door of my heart, You come in a greater way. I ask You to be Lord and Savior of my life, of my family, of all my affairs. Thank You, Heavenly Father. Thank You, Jesus. Thank You, Holy Spirit.*

We open our hearts mainly through consent. What changed your life the day you married? Consent. You said, "I do," and you were never the same again. Consent opens the door to your heart. In every Eucharist we ask for the grace to say "Yes." It is a gift of God by which we can rise above our selfishness. A self-centered person would say, "Don't let the Lord get His hands on your life. You keep control." We say, "Lord, give me the grace to break through that selfishness and ask You to be Lord of my life."

When we recite the *Creed* we are asking for the grace to continue saying "Yes" at deeper and deeper levels. Every day we must say "Yes" to our Father.

Every day we must say "Come, Holy Spirit, fill my heart; enkindle in me a new fire of Your love. Melt me, mold me, fill me, use me. Come, Holy Spirit."

When we say the *Creed* we are saying with the apostle Paul, "I live now, not I, but Christ lives in me." We are saying, "Father, I want to be more open to your Holy Spirit, to your life that is within me." This is the key to the Christian life and the secret of health and wholeness: Saying "Yes" to the Father who has said "Yes" to us in so many marvelous and unbelievable ways.

When we profess our faith through the *Creed* we are doing our part to offset the atheistic, pagan teachings in our society. The Blessed Virgin Mary asked the young visionaries of Medjugorje to recite the *Creed* daily to offset the atheistic teachings they received in public schools. We say it once a week—hopefully with great attention and devotion.

When we articulate the *Creed* we open ourselves to the Holy Spirit and renew our baptismal promises and confirmation vows. Now the Holy Spirit can move into our spirit in a greater way, a more intense way. We have freed the Holy Spirit to flow in a powerful way. Let's be open to the healing power of this great prayer of the Church.

Altar Call

After professing our faith we will later answer an altar call when the priest invites us to receive the whole Jesus Christ into our hearts. More than other Christians, Catholics make an altar call each Sunday at Holy Communion. This one realization can bring great healing to any congregation.

Healing Reflections

* To believe, in the biblical sense, is to commit ourselves completely to the Lord. Recall the time you

said your deepest "Yes" to Him and thank Him.

* Take five minutes of quiet time now. Ask the Holy Spirit to possess you and to speak to your heart. Listen. Respond.

-12-

Prayer of the Faithful

The 'common prayer' or 'prayer of the faithful' is to be restored after the gospel and the homily, especially on Sundays and holy days of obligation. By this prayer in which the people are to take part, intercession will be made for the holy Church, for the civil authorities, for all those oppressed by various needs, for all mankind, and for the salvation of the entire world. [1]

The Lord is saying to the Church today, "...I have searched among them for someone who could build a wall or stand in the breach before me to keep me from destroying the land; but I found no one" (Ezek 22:30). He tells us in Galatians 6:2 to "Help carry one another's burdens; in that way you will fulfill the law of Christ." To 'bear' means to lift with the idea of removing. As intercessors we are agreeing to help carry the burden of another until it is released. Intercession is a holy calling in the Body of Christ.

As previously mentioned, I have distributed 50,000 prayer cards with the request that people pray for my ministry 15 minutes a week. When great healings take place in my services, I know they come about because my intercessors were faithful in prayer. I take to heart Paul's word, "At every opportunity pray in the Spirit, using prayers and petitions of every sort..." (Eph 6:18). I deeply value my intercessors.

For Whom Should We Pray?

Jesus calls us to pray for the world in crisis; to intercede for leaders of nations, church and civil authorities. He tells us to cry out for the conversion of people running the abortion clinics. He calls us to pray for the communications media, that those in charge will present uplifting, edifying films and shows. He calls us to pray for those who have been abused sexually, physically and verbally; that they will not act out their frustrations, pain and anger on other people; that they will be healed. He calls us to pray for reconciliation in families; for husbands to be true husbands of wives, fulfilling their responsibilities as heads of families—not with superiority, but accepting themselves as men of God. He calls us to pray for wives to be women of God—faithful, inspiring, loving wives. He calls us to pray for parents to inspire their children, teaching by their lifestyles. He calls us to pray for our children to be filled with the love of Jesus and not corrupted or seduced by the evil in the world. He calls us to pray that our children will meet Jesus as Lord and Savior. He calls us to pray for priests that they become men of deep prayer; to pray for vocations to the priesthood.

Pray for Vocations

"Bishop Fulton Sheen talked about two altar boys serving Mass. One of them did something stupid and the priest turned around and said, 'Get out of here and never come back.' That young boy never did come back. His name was Tito, the great leader of Yugoslavia; and what a loss he was to the Church.

"The other altar boy lived in Peoria, Illinois and one day served Mass for the bishop in the cathedral. The poor kid dropped a cruet of wine at the Offertory. Sheen remarked that there is nothing comparable, short of an atomic explosion, to the sound of a crystal cruet shattering against a marble floor. The bishop helped clean up and then finished the Mass. Afterward he said, 'Did you ever think about becoming a priest?' The boy said 'Yes.' 'Then I think you shall be a priest and go to Louvain someday for your studies.' The boy went home and talked to his mother who told him that Louvain was the Catholic University of Belgium. Later on John Fulton Sheen did study for the priesthood at Louvain and became Bishop, and eventually Archbishop, Fulton J. Sheen.

"God was reaching out to touch both boys at the Eucharist. One priest got in the way and interfered with God's call; the other focused lovingly and compassionately on who was serving his Mass, not the somewhat dramatic accident that happened." [2]

"The harvest is rich but the workers are few; therefore ask the harvest-master to send workers to His harvest" (Lk 10:2). Let's make prayers for vocations a daily part of our commitment!

Pray for Specific Needs

After making our general intercessions we can pray for specific needs of a few people in church that day. We should pray for everyone in the world, then pray for a few people in the congregation in pain. Often during Mass there are people who wish the priest would hurry and finish because they are in great pain. Sometimes in my healing Masses I will ask a few members of the congregation who are in pain to come up to the front for prayer. When we come together as two or more, there is enormous power generated. "Where two or three are gathered in my name, there am I in their midst" (Mt 18:20). If there are 500 people present, then we are touching the person in pain with 500 "volts" of Jesus' healing love. The more people praying, the more spiritual energy is generated. Many people who are open can be healed then. This is the experience of some priests who have had the courage to step forward and rely on the scripture that says, "...the sick upon whom they lay their hands will recover" (Mk 16:18).

We are called to have sympathy for alcoholics,

street people, people with AIDS. "There but for the grace of God go I." Psychologists tell us that our whole psychological orientation was mostly formed by age six months to two years. We can be working against a stream of influences implanted at an early age. We have inherited dispositions that come from our mothers in the womb. We need to be people of sympathy and compassion who lift up our suffering sisters and brothers in intercessory prayer. The Lord reminds us, "If you want to avoid judgment, stop passing judgment" (Mt 7:1). Have the mind of Jesus. Let His mind be in you.

We all have to undergo the suffering of living in an imperfect world. Whatever we do in word or deed, we can do it in the name of Jesus. When Mass is over, we can continue to be intercessors. Put on the eyes of faith when looking at an annoying person in the grocery line. See him through the eyes of Jesus. You have no idea what he has gone through. Offer your laundry time up to Jesus. Offer the time in line at the post office, or the bank, up to Jesus. Pray the rosary at the red light or while waiting for rush hour traffic to move, or the accident to be cleared on the freeway. Offer up your 5-10-20-30 acts of inconvenience each day in a "specific" way—for example, for your unhappy son, your overworked pastor, your aunt with cancer. Interceding for needy people is truly doing penance.

A mother who has prayed for years for her children can expect their conversion, even if it is after her death. I hear many stories such as, "I have an aunt who prayed for me for years...a mother...a brother who prayed." We hear testimonies about how "The Lord touched me; I threw down the drink; I was converted." The real source of the conversion may be grandma who died of cancer, offering up her suffering for her grandchildren. We have the infinite power of God available through the power of prayer and faith. I know a woman whose two grown daughters were on drugs. One almost died from a gunshot wound. After years of the mother's persistent prayers, both daughters now live moral lives.

Survey Responses

In the survey the question was asked, "For whom do you pray at Mass?" Most respondents said "self," "children" and "spouse." Relationships were at the top of the list in prayer concerns, with "unforgiveness" a major contender for healing in those situations. Spiritual problems, health and money were the basic areas of concern.

The respondents were asked to write a simple prayer that they might commonly pray at Mass. A few representative responses include:

* Lord please heal my children, grandchildren and husband and bring them to yourself. Send a Christian friend to minister to them as they won't listen to me. (Bernadette M.)

* Lord I pray that our government leaders might have the wisdom and serenity to make the correct decisions. (Alicia Matheus)

* Lord, make Your presence known to these people. Soften their hearts that they can come to You without fear and distrust. Draw them closer to You that they may experience all the wonderful things You have for them. (Sue Cevasco)

* Lord please give Your abundant grace and love to my sick daughter- in-law Cora. (Virginia Zandueta)

* I lift up to You, Lord, the homeless, the poor and the sick. Give them warmth, shelter, food and healing. Thank You, Lord. Amen. (Carmelita Wolfert)

* Lord Jesus, touch my little girl in a powerful way;

take control of her life and make her the person You want her to be. Guide her and walk beside her. (Matti Hyatt)

* Lord, please open my brother Ken's heart that he may accept the gift of salvation and be delivered from drugs and alcohol. (Rodger S.)

* Dear Jesus, please pour Your Precious Blood over David to heal him of his alcoholism and help him know that he is loved. (Paul Robert)

* Dear Lord Jesus, please help my wife cope, for she has so many burdens to bear. Shower her with your healing grace and carry her spirit when she stumbles. (Edward Popielarski)

* Lord, protect Your priests. In this day of materialism and temptations, may Your priests feel Your presence and experience Your healing love. Ignite within them the fire of Your love so that they may love as You love. (Muriel Neveux)

* In the name of Jesus I cover these people with Your Precious Blood. I cover their minds, thoughts and emotions, body, soul and spirit. I seal them in Your Blood. Amen. (Frances Phillips)

* Abba, Father, in Jesus' name I pray for a miracle healing from lupus for my daughter Candy. You know Lord that without this she may not be able to have children or even live very long. Jesus, I put this prayer in Your Sacred Heart. Just as the woman with the issue of blood touched the hem of Your garment and was totally healed, I believe that through my faith you will heal Candy. Thank You, Lord. Amen. (Betty Dubuisson)

* I pray that my father will be converted and be faithful to mom. (Amy)

* Father in heaven, Holy Spirit, Jesus, watch over my wife and children. Increase their faith. Give me a helping hand to do the right things in life. Thank You for Your past help. (Jim Franke)

* Lord, I hunger for Your touch. Help me through the next week. Give me direction. Thank You for continuing to work with me even when I have failed. (Jerry Weibel)

* Lord, I lift up to You the people who have hurt me in my life. Please forgive them, and forgive me for causing them pain. (Judy Labaria)

* I pray that my son would be guided by You, Lord, because at this young age he can be easily pulled by the bad spirit. (Ann Belale)

* God, I know that in Your power I can forgive my dad. Please heal our relationship through this Mass. (Rosario A.)

* Lord, be mindful of Guy. Send Your power strongly upon him that he might meet this current difficulty. (John Heilman)

Mystical Mass Prayer
by Father Luke Zimmer

"Eternal Father, we offer to You, through the Immaculate and Sorrowful Heart of Mary, in the Holy Spirit, the Body, Blood, Soul and Divinity of our Lord Jesus Christ, in union with each Mass celebrated today and every day until the end of time. With Mother Mary, St. Joseph, each angel and saint in heaven, each soul in purgatory, each person in the Body of Christ and the family of God, we offer each act of love, adoration, praise and worship. We offer each act of thanksgiving for blessings, graces and gifts received. We offer each act of reparation for sins that have been, are being and will be committed until the end of time. And we offer each act of intercessory prayer. We offer all of these prayers in union with Jesus in each Mass celebrated throughout the world.

We stand before You, Triune God, like the prodigal son asking to be accepted, like the publican asking for mercy and forgiveness, like the paralytic asking for healing and strength, and like the good thief asking for salvation. We consecrate ourselves and all creation to You.

Eternal Father, we ask You in the name of Jesus, through the power of His Precious Blood, through His death on the cross, through His resurrection and ascension, to send forth the Holy Spirit upon all mankind.

Holy Spirit, we ask for an outpouring of Your graces, blessings and gifts; upon those who do not believe that they may believe; upon those who are doubtful or confused, that they may understand; upon those who are lukewarm or indifferent, that they may be transformed; upon those who are constantly living in a state of sin, that they may be converted; upon those who are weak, that they may be strengthened; upon those who are holy, that they may persevere.

We ask You to bless our Holy Father. Give him strength and health in body, soul and spirit. Bless his ministry and make it fruitful. Protect him from his enemies.

Bless each cardinal, bishop, priest, brother, sister and all aspiring to the religious life, especially _____ and grant many the gift of a vocation to the priesthood and religious life.

Bless each member of our families, relatives and friends, especially _____. Bless the poor, the sick, the underprivileged, the dying and all those in need, especially _____.

Bless those who have died and are in a state of purification, that they may be taken to heaven, especially _____.

We offer and consecrate ourselves and all creation to you, Heart of Jesus, Mary and Joseph. We ask you,

Mary and Joseph, to take us with all our hopes and desires. Please offer them with Jesus in the Holy Spirit to our Heavenly Father, in union with each Mass offered throughout all time.

We consecrate ourselves to Archangel Michael, Gabriel and Raphael, and each angel, especially our guardian angel. We ask in the name of Jesus, through our mother Mary, queen of all angels, that You, O Heavenly Father, send forth legions of angels to minister to us.

Archangel Michael with his legions to ward off the attacks of the world, the flesh and the devil; Archangel Gabriel with his legions to teach us that we may know and do Your will, and they may help us to catechize and evangelize; Archangel Raphael with his legions to heal our woundedness, supply for our limitations, strengthen us in our weakness, to overcome demonic depression, to give us joy in the spirit, to protect us in our travels and to supply for all our needs.

Finally, we ask for the gift of unconditional love, that we can live the love-life that was reflected in the Holy Family at Nazareth, thus bringing about justice and peace throughout the world. Amen." [3]

Healing Reflections

* Do you pray for healing for yourself at the "Prayers of the Faithful?"

* Do you promise to pray for others at the "Prayers of the Faithful?" Why not?

* If you were to see people visibly healed at the "Prayers of the Faithful," do you think other people would start attending Mass more?

PART IV

LITURGY OF THE EUCHARIST

*The renewal in the Eucharist of the covenant
between the Lord and man draws the faithful into
the compelling love of Christ and sets them afire.*[1]

Presentation of the Gifts

During the presentation of the gifts, representatives of the lay community bring up the bread and wine and other gifts to be received with the collection. They are all our gifts given back to God. The gifts of bread and wine, representing all of us, will be transformed into the real presence of Jesus Christ as His Body and Blood, soul and divinity.

Collection

Linda Schubert shared that she was sitting in church one day when a friend came over and sat nearby. As the friend prayed, the Lord asked Linda, "Does the $50 in your wallet belong to me?" Linda said, "Yes, Lord." He continued, "I want to give it to Carol." Her first impulse was to resist. Then she quickly repented, took out the money and turned to the woman. "Carol, the Lord just told me to give you this money." Carol began to cry, and said, "Yesterday I wrote a $45.00 check for groceries with no money in my account. I knew the check would bounce, but I had to have food for my children." Carol and Linda cried and hugged and prayed together. Carol left with new lightness in her step and a deep sense of being cared for by God. Linda reflected, "I drove home repenting of the times I had hardened my heart when I felt the Lord nudging me to give." "Oh, that today you would hear his voice; Harden not your hearts..." (Ps 95:7-8).

One of the hardest things for people to yield is their money. The Lord knows this, yet He tells us to tithe—to give 10% of our income to the Church. Malachi 3:10 says, "Bring the whole tithe into the storehouse, that there may be food in my house..." Our tithe is an expression of our total dependence upon God and our love for (and need of) our brothers and sisters. If we could tithe there would be no need for tuition in Catholic schools. There would be fewer street people, because we would be providing homes for them and taking care of their needs. There are many who are poor among us and dependent upon the parish for help. Our offering is meant to provide for the needy. Many people don't realize that the collection is an act of love and gratitude.

Giving tithes is also part of our worship. We have participated so far in an act of love in the Liturgy of the Word, and now as we begin the Liturgy of the Eucharist we acknowledge our dependence upon God for everything. In our giving we say, "Lord, I put You first." In our giving we say, "Lord, all is Yours," as in the prayer of St. Ignatius: "Take Lord, receive, all my liberty. My memory, my understanding, my entire will. All is Yours. You have given all to me, now I return it to You. Give me only Your love and Your grace. That's enough for me."

We are called to model ourselves after the widow who gave everything (Lk 21:2). She worshipped the Lord with her giving, demonstrating an open, loving heart. We are to worship the Lord with our resources, showing our openness of heart toward God and our brothers and sisters; revealing our trust. We place our resources in the "bank of heaven." "Do not lay up for yourselves an earthly treasure...store up heavenly treasure...for where your treasure is, there your heart is" (Mt 6:19-21). As we lose our possessiveness toward them, we give God a channel through which He can give to us. A woman in New Orleans married 25 years heard a talk on tithing at Mass and decided to try it. After one year she and her husband were debt free for the first time in their marriage.

Some preachers talk about seed faith, and expectation of returns on giving. We can learn from this teaching. Faithfulness in giving opens our hearts to receive what He wants to give. Jesus says, "Give, and it shall be given to you. Good measure, pressed down, shaken together, running over, will they pour into the fold of your garment. For the measure you measure with will be measured back to you" (Lk 6:38). When we give cheerfully, openly, courageously, freely and abundantly, we are then in a position to receive from God.

He wants to give back to us even more than we want to receive. He wants to give us that abundant life that He speaks of in John 10:10. He wants us to be happy. What do you need? Resources? Ideas? Wisdom? Health? The sky's the limit with the Lord. Ask Him to give you a vision and a dream for your life, and be open to the fulfillment. He may test you in your giving, but watch and see what He will do for you when you surrender all. The hardest test is the finances. Everything else seems somewhat easy in comparison.

Talk to God about your money. His share is holy. Make Him your partner. Plant your gifts like seeds in holy ground, then open your spirit and ask God for dividends on your investment and fulfillment of your visions and dreams. Expect to receive. A tremendous healing grace is released through giving. "Bring the whole tithe into the storehouse, that there may be food in My house, and try me in this, says the Lord of hosts: Shall I not open for you the floodgates of heaven, to pour down blessing upon you without measure? For your sake I will forbid the locust to destroy your crops; And the vine in the field will not be barren, says the Lord of hosts" (Mal 3:10-11).

Offertory

As the priest receives the gifts of the Christian community—bread, wine and the collection—we

should be mindful that we are now being called to give
not only our support, but our whole selves in the
offering of bread and wine to God.

The priest puts a little water in the wine after the
Jewish custom that can represent for us the melting of
ourselves into Jesus Christ in the Mass. As the water
disappears into the wine, we blend into Christ Jesus.

We offer all that we are—mind, soul and body. We
should offer all that we possess, including family,
health and marriage. Let's give them to the Lord now.
We must surrender them one day in death.

Just imagine that this was the last Mass you would
ever offer because of a terminal disease. What
surrender and abandonment would you feel at that
moment? Try to capture that affection and disposition
now at Mass. The last Mass that will be offered for us
will be our funeral Mass. Then it will be too late; we
will have passed into the light. If there is anything you
cannot surrender to the Lord, then you do not possess
it; it possesses you. All of us have something that we
find difficult or impossible to give. Let us ask the Lord
for His grace to give it to Him so He can bless it and
then give it back to us.

We come to Mass to unite ourselves to Jesus Christ
in His great sacrifice. There is tremendous healing
when we offer ourselves and make a sincere effort to be
one with Jesus. We hear much about satanism these
days. From experience we know that many people who
are obsessed with evil have invited it in, or opened
themselves to occult activity. The opposite is true for
us. The more we open ourselves to Jesus, the more His
Holy Spirit can possess and fill us. Each Mass is a
golden opportunity to become one with Jesus.

Healing Reflections

* How does God work in your life to detach you from
  possessiveness about your resources?

* What are you holding on to now, that He is calling
  you to release?

-14-

Consecration

Take this, all of you, and eat it; this is my body which will be given for you.

Take this, all of you, and drink from it; this is the cup of my blood, the blood of the new and everlasting covenant.

Do this in memory of me.

The consecration of the Mass should be seen in light of the gospel readings from John 14-16. These are some of the most beautiful chapters in the New Testament. We are called not only to service, but also to consecration. Jesus loves us. "I am indeed going to prepare a place for you, and then I shall come back to take you with me, that where I am you also may be" (Jn 14:3). "The Paraclete, the Holy Spirit whom the Father will send in My name, will instruct you in everything, and remind you of all that I told you" (Jn 14:26). These are but a few of the consolations Jesus gave to His apostles. This knowledge of His love is a prelude to the consecration of bread and wine. As bread and wine are transformed into Jesus' body and blood, there is a spiritual transformation in each person attending. One priest maintains that when the consecration takes place, there is a tremendous sweep of divine energy through the congregation. "Notice," he said, "how many people cough and sneeze then. This is negative energy being cleansed from people." It would stand to reason that at this most powerful moment the Holy Spirit would cleanse people.

Sister Briege's Prophecy

Sister Briege McKenna, O.S.C. at the priests' retreat at International Falls, Minnesota, on April 26, 1990, spoke this word she heard coming from the Lord: "Come to Me in My Eucharistic presence. There is a time coming in which there will be a great denial of My presence, denial that I am truly present among My people. But I invite you to spend time with Me. I invite you to lead your people to come to Me. There will flow life-giving waters. I will refresh you and free you. I will pray that angels protect you. I will give you My angels to go with you and before you. No one will rob you of what I have given you if you stay close to Me. Come and taste the Bread of Life. Invite your people to come and in this way you will prepare for the darkness that will come upon the Church. For evil forces will try to destroy my people. I invite you to come to Me often. Come and let Me cleanse you of your sinfulness. Do not accept the darkness in your own life. Do not allow yourself to be deceived. New life means that I love you, that I long to make you spotless. Come to Me often. Confess to one another and allow Me to minister through each other and I will give you the wisdom that you need to confront the enemy."

Father George Maloney's Reflections

To quote Father George Maloney, S.J.: "Eucharist: The peak of all Christian healing, especially in deeper faith, hope and love on a spiritual plane, should be found in our frequent and devout reception of the Holy Eucharist. It is the new covenant whereby God continually gives His blood for the remission of sins and the life of the world (Heb 9:15, 25-28). In this sacrament that, as priests, we bring to others and also receive each day in the divine liturgy, we approach

God, the consuming fire (Heb 12:29), with great expectancy...that the deep roots of sinfulness in us will be replaced with a new surge of God's eternal resurrectional life in us. Like the woman with the hemorrhage in the gospel story (Lk 8:43-44), we need only touch Jesus and His power will flow into us bringing new life.

"Of all the sacraments, the Eucharist is the climax because here Jesus Christ, the perfect Image of the Father, gives Himself unto eternal life. Here He conquers in that eternal now of self-immolation on the cross for love of us individually all sin and death that exist within us. Here we must experience a sharing in His glorious resurrection as His Spirit dissolves in us our lack of love for God and for neighbor." [1]

Father Walter Ciszek's Story

Father Walter J. Ciszek, S.J., was captured by the Russian army in World War II and spent 23 years in Soviet prisons and the labor camps of Siberia. It was only through his utter reliance on God's will that he managed to endure. In the following excerpt from his book, *He Leadeth Me*, he shares his deep reverence for the Mass.

"The danger and the difficulty of saying Mass became a reality for us in the lumber camps of the Urals. We began then to do what we probably should have done before: we began to prepare to say the Mass by heart...over and over again in the evenings...we would repeat to each other the prayers of the Mass until we had learned them by heart.

"Sometimes Father Victor and I would walk out into the forest and there offer Mass on a stump of a tree...even time seemed to stand still as we offered the eternal sacrifice of Calvary for the many intentions that filled our thoughts and our hearts, not the least of which was the thought of the deprived thousands of the Church of silence here in this once Christian land for whom we had come to work as priests in secret...at other times Father Victor and I would say Mass sitting on the edge of our beds across from one another. We pretended to be reading or talking softly as we said the Mass prayers. We could not use the chalice in the barracks, so our cup became a common drinking glass and our host a piece of leavened bread.

"...in the prison camps of Siberia the priests and prisoners would go to great lengths, run risks willingly, to have the consolation of this sacrament... In small groups the prisoners would shuffle into the assigned place, and there the priest would say Mass in his working clothes, unwashed, disheveled, bundled up against the cold. We said Mass in drafty storage shacks, or huddled in mud and slush in the corner of a building site foundation of an underground. The intensity of devotion of both priests and prisoners made up for everything: there were no altars, candles, bells, flowers, music, snow-white linens, stained glass or the warmth that even the simplest parish church could offer. Yet in these primitive conditions, the Mass brought you closer to God than anyone might conceivably imagine. The realization of what was happening on the board, box or stone used in place of an altar penetrated deep into the soul. Distractions caused by the fear of discovery, which accompanied each saying of the Mass under such conditions, took nothing away from the effect that the tiny bit of bread and few drops of consecrated wine produced upon the soul." 2

Visualization

Most of us will never face the situation encountered by the prisoners in Siberia, and thus won't have the opportunity to grow in that kind of testing ground. But we can learn by identifying with them in faith imagination. We can ask the Holy Spirit to bring the fruit of their experience into our lives.

Away from family and friends, without creature comforts, cold, without all the normal structure that we might call upon in place of Jesus, He is all we have.

We are gathered secretly in the forest, huddled around a priest in dirty work clothes offering a Mass on the stump of a tree. The wind is bitter cold and we move in close to keep each other warm.

As he lifts the bit of stale bread up to the Lord at the consecration a brilliant white light radiates out from the bread, the Body of Christ, to the hearts of His people huddled around the makeshift altar. The stream of white light is melting hurts that have accumulated over the years like a hard coat of shellac on our hearts—the negativity, the anger, the bitterness, the resentment. It is setting us free, replacing our hearts of stone with hearts of flesh.

Now let's see our hearts as Jesus sees them: tender, soft, open, surrendered, clean, free. Let's see ourselves as Jesus sees us: beautiful, beloved, whole, accepted, redeemed, washed in His blood, nourished with His Body and Blood, at one with the Body of Christ.

The Holy Spirit speaks in the language of visions, dreams and imagination. God brings things into being in our lives through the use of our imaginations. God spoke in visions and dreams with Abraham in Genesis 13 and with Jacob in Genesis 30. He gave Peter the image of himself as a rock, and he became that rock. In Ramona's story (Chapter 9) tremendous healing came through active imagination guided by the Holy Spirit.

Carl Simonton, M.D., wrote *Getting Well Again* that outlines his work in visualization with terminally ill cancer patients. Through x-rays he shows the patients their cancer, then has them visualize an army of white blood cells overwhelming the cancer cells and destroying them. He has a high percentage of cures with terminally ill patients as he combines this program with other things including meditation and forgiveness. His main approach centers on visualization.

Muriel's Experience

Muriel Neveux shared, "The Lord directed me to bring those I needed to forgive to the Eucharist. As the priest held up the host during the consecration I saw the face of each person on the host. I asked the Lord to heal the relationships because they, too, were part of His body. I also asked Him to make it palatable at the time I received the Eucharist."

Healing Reflections

* Do I pray to realize the incredible mystery taking place in every Mass?

* How would I focus on the consecration if I knew this were to be my last Mass?

* What can I do to deepen my faith in the consecration of the Mass?

* Do I attend Mass as often as possible?

* Does television mean more to me than the Holy Mass?

Communion Rite

The Lord's Prayer

We are invited to stand and pray to our Heavenly Father with Jesus, Mary and the saints, as He taught us. In this chapter we will explore ways of entering more deeply into the healing power of *The Lord's Prayer.* Regular meditation on this prayer will increase sensitivity to the healing our Father wants to accomplish in and through our lives.

This is a prayer of relationship. Some people lift up their hands as they pray, communicating to God their openness, their surrender, and perhaps their desire to be touched by Him. In many parishes the people join hands to build a sense of community, although some people can't do this. Some are so wounded and broken, perhaps physically or sexually abused, that they can't accept the touch of another person.

We approach the Lord in the attitude of repentance and humility, realizing our poverty of spirit while also rejoicing in the knowledge that we are sons and daughters, heirs to the kingdom. We are, "A chosen race, a royal priesthood, a holy nation, a people He claims for His own to proclaim the glorious works of the One who called you from darkness into His marvelous light" (1Pet 2:9).

Jesus taught us to call God our Father, and so we have the courage to say:

OUR FATHER...As we say the words "Our Father," we are going to Him arm in arm with our brothers and sisters around the world. And we are remembering in our prayers those who have died. God is "our" Father, the Father of the living and the dead.

God, the great "I Am," has chosen to be our Father. He has chosen to create, nurture, teach, heal, provide for, protect, discipline and love each of us. He holds us in the palm of His hand and promises never to leave or forsake us. The same God who dwells in the highest heaven asks us to call Him "Father" and invites us into an intimate relationship with Him.

I must confess that even after 25 years of Catholic education I still considered God as judge until the Holy Spirit touched me in a powerful way. Then I began to recognize God as loving Father. Many people still see God as someone to be feared, because they have been formed in a negative Christianity where God is judge, rather than the positive New Testament Christianity that focuses on love, acceptance and forgiveness. Also, we generally learn about God as Father through the model of our earthly father. Many struggles in life are related to our relationship with our fathers. When this relationship is not right we spend our lives in an endless search. Some people lash out at others in a negative way; some search for healing; most struggle for approval. As we open ourselves to experience the approval of Father God, a deep sense of wholeness and relaxation settles into our spirits.

Sister Stephanie Weber of Yankton, South Dakota shares her healing about praying to God the Father in the following story.

Sister Stephanie's Story

"When I was given the job of assistant executive director of a home for troubled girls, I took a class to develop my counseling skills. During the training my therapist said one day, 'I perceive you are angry with your father.' 'I can't touch that!' I replied sharply. So we proceeded to work on some angers I could touch. For me to be angry with someone was to deny love. I knew I loved my father deeply.

"At another therapy session he said, 'I perceive that you have not buried your father.' (He had been dead for six years.) We did a burial exercise. In visualization we dug a grave, placed a coffin in the ground and covered it. From then on I could visualize the grave closed, not above the ground as it had been as I walked away on the day of the funeral.

"A year or so later, after I had relocated to another teaching assignment, I found myself still dealing with a lot of anger and frustration. My sister suggested that I go to a Christmas retreat at Pecos, New Mexico, and offered me her reservation. I accepted.

"On the third day of the retreat I had a conference with the retreat director. I expressed to him my state of confusion and inability to pray. At one point the priest said, 'Sister, I perceive you are angry with your father.' 'I can't touch that,' I responded once more. When I told him about the burial exercise he said, 'You only succeeded in burying him deeper into your subconscious. You still have not buried him.'

"He talked a bit and then asked me if I ever prayed to God the Father. That was my moment of truth. I wanted to say, 'Yes, I have said *The Our Father* thousands of times.' The Holy Spirit kept me honest. I finally said, 'I have said *The Our Father* thousands of times, but to pray to the Father, no. I pray to Jesus and Mary.' He said it would have been difficult for him to believe me if I had said 'Yes,' for my concept of father was that of a man I could never please. Since our only concept of God the Father is the concept we have of our own natural father, he felt it would be impossible for me to pray to a God I believed I could not please.

"I know from reflection that this belief about my father came from the tape I continued to play in my mind—statements that my mother made when she didn't want us to do certain things. She would say such things as, 'Don't do that, you are the daughter of Steve W...Don't do that, you will displease your father...Don't do that, you will disgrace your father.' Mom put my father on a pedestal. She had been so put down by her stepmother that my father's love for her qualified him for sainthood.

"The priest at Pecos prayed for me for the healing of all my relationships, from childhood to the present, especially with my parents, brothers and sisters. The words he spoke at the end of the prayer are indelibly written on my mind: 'Now, Heavenly Father, please give her the grace to put the hand of her father into Your hand and let him rest in peace. Amen.'

"Wow! I received a flood of joy and peace. That prayer was said fifteen years ago, and remains present like a deep river flowing below the rest of my life and activities. It is astounding to me how easily and freely I have been able to pray to my Heavenly Father since then."

The foundation of healing in *The Lord's Prayer* is the deep truth that God is loving Father. "God is love" (1Jn 4:16). We are safe in Him. We can entrust our lives to Him. He is faithful, trustworthy and reliable in every way. The word "Abba," loving Father, is used 175 times in the New Testament. The first healing we can expect to encounter in the Lord's Prayer is the knowledge that God is loving Father.

WHO ART IN HEAVEN...This phrase reminds us that He is not like our earthly fathers. His love is perfect and unconditional. He will never hurt us. He will never let us down. He is all that we need. He wants to help us in every way, even in small matters of everyday living. His resources are unlimited. He is able to perform mighty acts of healing and deliverance to meet our every need. His ways are higher than ours. Yet we can know Him, and walk with Him in heavenly realms. "...set your heart on what pertains to higher realms..." (Col 3:1).

HALLOWED BE THY NAME...God's name (His nature, His person, His character) is holy, set apart from defilement and worthy of all reverence. We pray that His name be held holy in our lives and in the lives of all people. We pray to live so that His name is always honored.

The more we can praise His holiness, His wonderful nature, the more open we are to healing. On Pentecost Sunday the Holy Spirit confirmed on the 120 the gift of tongues to praise the Father in a more powerful way. He still gives the gift of praise in tongues today. We have a loving Father whose name is Holy. Let us praise Him with all our hearts.

THY KINGDOM COME, THY WILL BE DONE ON EARTH AS IT IS IN HEAVEN... We are asking Him to rule in our personal lives, and in the world to come. Say, "Lord, confirm Your kingship over me." "You are my King and my God" (Ps 44:5). We pray that His justice and peace reign in the hearts of all people. We pray that His kingdom will come in the midst of countries at war. We pray that His kingdom will come in the midst of the people on drugs, and in the abortion clinics. We pray for His kingdom to come in broken families, broken bodies, broken lives.

As we mature in our Christian journey it becomes clear that our primary purpose is to help build that kingdom right where we are. For each of us there is a specific task according to our vocation. As Christians, to do the will of the Father and complete His work is as important to our spiritual well-being as food is to our body. True happiness comes in surrender to the will of God. "To do Thy will, O my God, is my delight" (Ps 40:9).

GIVE US THIS DAY OUR DAILY BREAD...God has always supplied the needs of His people, through ordinary and extraordinary means. He provided for the Israelites in the desert (Ex 16-17); He provided food for Elijah and the widow who served him (1Kgs 17:7-15); He fed the 5,000 (Lk 9:10-17).

There are many modern-day examples, including that of Father Rick Thomas' community and their experience of multiplication of food for the poor in Juarez, Mexico, as recorded in *Miracles in El Paso?* by Rene Laurentin. In 1975 Carole Raymond was making tortillas and the sack from which she was scooping the corn flour did not diminish in proportion to the amount she was taking out. Father Rick Thomas reported the multiplication of grapes from the Lord's Ranch in July 1977. There are also reports of multiplication of avocados and tortillas in 1977, cans of milk in 1978, and squash in 1980. [1]

We come to the Lord with daily needs of body, mind and spirit. We pray for physical needs: shelter, clothing, food, health. We pray for the needs of our minds: knowledge of divine things, education, learning, guidance and wisdom in decision-making, social needs, emotional and mental health. We pray for the needs of our spirits: our relationship with God, the grace of forgiveness, deeper conversion and the ability to carry out our particular vocation in life.

Jesus told the story of the vineyard owner who hired workers at different hours and paid them all the same wage. He gave each what was needed for the day. We all have the same fundamental needs; He gives us what we need for the day.

FORGIVE US OUR TRESPASSES AS WE FORGIVE THOSE WHO TRESPASS AGAINST US...Forgiveness is the next key element of healing in *The Lord's Prayer.* If you have trouble forgiving, ask God to help you to be willing to forgive. You may find it helpful to meditate upon the scriptures dealing with the mercy of God, the Passion, and the prodigal son. These will help you experience the Father's forgiveness and love. Know that the Father is always waiting with open arms. Let us respond to His love today.

AND LEAD US NOT INTO TEMPTATION...Jesus went through an ordeal of temptation in the desert before the start of His ministry (Mt 4:1-11). Satan tempted Jesus just the same way he tempts us, offering us all the riches and power of the world if we will but follow him. Jesus knew the battle we would have in this world. He prayed to His Father on behalf of His disciples and all of us. He knows our weaknesses and vulnerabilities to temptation and will reveal the path to victory.

Taking Charge of Temptations

Temptations can begin in the mind and be carried out through the senses. When the thoughts first come, we need to take charge of them before they are deeply implanted. If we allow sinful thoughts to take root in our minds they will grow and we will eventually succumb to temptation. Offer up the temptation and ask the Lord for the gift of holiness instead.

We can, like Jesus, use scripture to battle temptations. It is helpful to write down and meditate on the scriptures that best combat specific temptations. Paul tells us, "...be transformed by the renewal of your mind..." (Rom 12:2). Philippians 4:8-9 tells us to direct our thoughts toward all that is "...honest, pure, admirable, decent, virtuous or worthy of praise."

Another important pathway to victory is through the Eucharist. Bring the temptation to the Lord during the Mass, and release it to him during the Eucharist.

It is also helpful when temptations are deeply implanted to receive special prayer for healing and discernment. Having the support of others, especially in small group situations, is very healing.

Overcoming temptations is an ongoing process. One of the most important rules of the spiritual life is to rise if we ever do succumb to temptation.

BUT DELIVER US FROM EVIL...this is a powerful prayer of deliverance. Some translations say, "Deliver (or save) us from the evil one." This was the form used in the early Church. We can be delivered from evil. We can call upon Jesus and He will come in power. We do not have to be entrapped and ensnared by the enemy. Every time we are about to fall, we can call upon Him and He will be there.[2]

We might look at evil in the broader sense as anything that prevents us from experiencing the love of God. We ask for deliverance from feelings of unworthiness and anxiety. Our Lord says, "Do not be anxious." What is anxiety but a concern about the future? It is worry about the future over which we have no control. Deliver us from every evil. Help us with our inclinations to worry, our tendency to give in to things that take us away from God; to resent; to seek revenge. This is death producing. We ask for life. Say, "Lord, I will stand firm in Your strength."

Jesus tells us in James 4:7 that we are to resist the devil and he will flee. We seek God's divine protection through prayer, taking authority over evil, through scripture, through the sacraments, through Christian community.

We don't need to be afraid of evil. We are walking with our Heavenly Father, in the name of Jesus, in the power of the Holy Spirit. "...For there is One greater in you than there is in the world" (1Jn 4:4).

When we pray *The Lord's Prayer* we are united with millions of others around the world who pray this prayer every day. Conscious of these facts we stand humbly before the Father with Jesus, Mary and the saints, taking our rightful place as sons and daughters of our loving Father and boldly proclaim:

> *Our Father who art in heaven, hallowed be thy name.*
>
> *Thy kingdom come, Thy will be done on earth as it is in heaven.*
>
> *Give us this day our daily bread. Forgive us our trespasses as we forgive those who trespass against us and lead us not into temptation but deliver us from evil.*

FOR THINE IS THE KINGDOM, AND THE POWER AND THE GLORY FOREVER. AMEN!

Healing Reflections

For those who have difficulty relating to God as loving Father, the following steps may be helpful:

1. Ask for the grace to be healed of past hurts dealing with your father.

2. Reflect upon the three greatest hurts.

3. Expect that there will be healing.

4. Seek prayer from someone familiar with this type of healing process.

5. Pray *The Forgiveness Prayer* found in Chapter 4.

6. Pray for your father, whether living or dead. If he is living, pray blessings upon him. Place no conditions on your prayer.

7. Praise and thank God for your father, whether living or dead, whether you have good feelings or bad feelings about him. Praise is a decision not a feeling.

8. Search the scriptures and write down all the verses that speak to you about God the Father's personal love and care.

9. Repeat these scriptures daily and let them become a part of you.

10. Seek spiritual direction.

The Sign of Peace

Lord Jesus Christ, You said to Your apostles: I leave you peace, my peace I give you. Look not on our sins, but on the faith of Your Church, and grant us the peace and unity of Your kingdom where You live for ever and ever.

The sign of peace says, in non-verbal and verbal

ways, "I love you." We are saying, "I want my relationship with God to flow through all my other relationships." The following story from World War I is a powerful testimony of the desire in the human heart for peace.

Miracle in World War I

During the First World War Europe was a political tinderbox. The armies of France, Britain, Russia, Germany and Austria-Hungary began a war that would claim millions of lives. But a little-known miracle took place on Christmas Day, 1914. It was a miracle of human kindness and love.

In November of that year Pope Benedict XV called for a cessation of hostilities on Christ's birthday. Both sides said, "Impossible." What seemed impossible to those in high places is possible for ordinary soldiers, however, who often long for peace and home. The thousands of soldiers facing each other in the trenches that stretched from the Swiss border to the North Atlantic decided to call off the war themselves.

At sundown on Christmas Eve the firing died slowly until every gun was silent. According to reports, it was a young British soldier who first sensed that a miracle had occurred. Standing guard at midnight in an isolated outpost, Peter Goudge heard the German troops singing "Stille Nacht, Heilige Nacht." Goudge started singing too. Before long, English and Irish troops began singing "O Come, All Ye Faithful." The singing continued until, all along the Western Front, former enemies were singing Christmas carols with joy and peace in their hearts.

English and Irish troops then noticed hundreds of colored lights strung up by the German soldiers along the barbed wire fence in front of their trenches. At intervals along the trenches brightly colored Christmas trees brought the solemnity of the season to the war-ravaged battleground. One lone German soldier leaned over the barbed wire of the British trenches and shouted in English, "Merry Christmas."

Soon the air was filled with shouts of "Merry Christmas" and "Froeliche Weihnachten."

The Germans then shouted, "Come out—we will not shoot for Christmas." Troops climbed out of their trenches and advanced unarmed to greet yesterday's enemies. Some laughed, others were near tears as they embraced. The Christmas spirit caught on quickly along the hundreds of miles of trenches. French troops shouted "Joyeux Noel" and a band serenaded the German troops with classical music. Belgian and German troops exchanged gifts of cigars and cheese given by loved ones at home. The spirit of Christmas overcame all. Toasts with beer and wine or tea and coffee were offered for home and family and friends. The most popular toast was to peace.

The only serious business on this day involved burying the dead. Both sides dug graves for those who had fallen, and the British supplied some wooden crosses. Then a party of Germans moved toward the British lines, carrying the body of a British soldier who had fallen behind their lines.

As evening fell, soldiers began to trickle back to their trenches reluctantly to resume the bitter business at hand. Tears and embraces marked the parting of thousands of soldiers who at last had found "peace on earth, good will toward men"—if only for a day.

The military high commands of both sides took severe measures to insure that warring troops would not repeat such an event in the future. [3]

Peace Begins with Ourselves

Sometimes we come to church and pray for peace in the world while we are not at peace with ourselves, or our families and friends. Yet it must start close to home.

One of the most powerful ways we are healed is by being loved by other people. As we share with them our fears and disappointments; as we forgive each other; as we see goodness in them; as we love; as we are at peace with ourselves and those in our inner circle, then we will find healing. There is tremendous potential for healing as we gather together in community.

The sign of peace is not a social time, a time to run all over the church talking to friends. It is a time to express that Christian love to those on either side, lovingly, reverently, as representatives of the whole community. Because communion is a sign of our union with God and one another, we offer a sign of peace to those around us at that time. People tend to be drawn out of the reverence of the moment during the sign of peace, however. I will sometimes move it to the end of the penitential rite to avoid this situation. Either way is acceptable.

The great commandment is to love one another. In the Mass, we express this by our sign of peace. It is said that Catholics are "God's frozen chosen." However, we thaw out to some degree by sharing a sign of peace in the Banquet of Love.

A Mother's Story

"It was hard to attend my son's first communion because of our painful family circumstances. I was divorced and my ex-husband sat with his girlfriend in the family section. I stayed towards the back, fighting tears and wishing I could leave. As I turned to greet the people in my vicinity during the sign of peace, a gray-haired woman took my hand in hers and said gently, 'Oh my dear, keep up your courage. You are doing just fine.' They were the most perfect words anyone could have said. This gentle stranger, who apparently knew about my circumstances, gave me fresh courage and hope. Jesus knew all about my pain and probably prompted her to sit behind me and pray for me during my son's first communion. Jesus reached out to heal me that day, through that woman." (N.W.)

Healing Reflections

* Jesus tells us that what we do to others, we do to Him. When you give the sign of peace at Mass this week, ask Jesus to give you a glimpse of Himself in each one you greet. Let the warmth of your greeting tell him/her that you really care.

* Think of one time that the sign of peace was very special for you. In what way?

Breaking of the Bread

> *Lamb of God, you take away the sins of the world: have mercy on us.*
>
> *Lamb of God, you take away the sins of the world: have mercy on us.*
>
> *Lamb of God, you take away the sins of the world: grant us peace.*

Linda Mitchell of Sunnyvale, California experiences powerful healing during this time of the Mass. She speaks of coming to Mass with a sense of helplessness in life situations, unable to change herself or others. She brings these circumstances to the Lord, lays them in the chalice and releases them during the consecration.

"During Mass I give to Jesus the particular helplessness, problem and situation. Through admitting my helplessness over the situation, the thought, the memory, the circumstance, He transforms the powerlessness into joy, strength and courage. He reassures me that I am loved, just the way I am. He reassures me that He will take care of the problem. I can rest in His love, knowing that He is in charge of things. Deep within I hear the words, 'I am changing your heart. I pour my love upon you and heal you.'

"I find that a simple act of trust and acceptance that Eucharist is Christ is the first step. Christ Himself will change my heart of stone to a heart of love. This is a love that is unknown to man by his own labor; it is a love beyond description and imagination; a love that all of us desire, deep, deep inside. The deepest desire of our heart is to receive that love because we have been created to receive that love. Each has a special place in the Father's heart. In that special place He waits for us. In Eucharist the deep need for love can be filled. We are designed to be in the Father's heart. In Eucharist our hearts can be cleansed from pain suffered. In Eucharist He washes away the hurt of childhood. Eucharist is the key to wholeness and holiness.

"The experience of Eucharist is individual, personal, and uniquely designed for each one of His children."

Lord Jesus Christ, with faith in Your love and mercy, I eat Your Body and drink Your Blood. Let it not bring me condemnation, but health in mind and body.

Communion

This is the Lamb of God who takes away the sins of the world. Happy are those who are called to His supper.

Father Walter J. Ciszek, S.J., in his story, *He Leadeth Me*, reflects on the reverence for the Mass by some prisoners in the labor camps: "...I have seen priests pass up breakfast and work at hard labor on an empty stomach until noon in order to keep the Eucharistic fast, because the noon break at the work site was the time we could best get together for a hidden Mass...sometimes, when the guards were observing us too closely and we couldn't risk saying Mass at the work site, the crusts of bread I had put in my pocket at breakfast remained there uneaten until I could get back to camp and say Mass at night...I have seen priests and prisoners deprive their bodies of needed sleep in order to get up before the rising bell for a secret Mass in a quiet barracks...In some ways, we led a catacomb existence with our Masses. We would be severely punished if we were discovered saying Mass, and there were always informers. But the Mass to us was always worth the danger and the sacrifice; we treasured it, we looked forward to it, we would do almost anything in order to say or to attend a Mass." 4

The Lanciano Miracle

In about the year 700, a Basilian monk in Lanciano, Italy, doubted the real presence of the Lord in the Eucharist. Father Stefano Manelli in *Jesus Our Eucharistic Love*, tells the story: "He could not bring himself to believe that at the words of consecration uttered by him over bread and wine, their substances became the Body and Blood of Christ. But being a devout priest he continued to celebrate the sacrament according to the teaching of the Church and begged God to remove the doubt.

"One day, as he was offering the Holy Sacrifice, following the words of consecration, the bread literally changed into Flesh and the wine into Blood. At first he was overwhelmed by what he saw. Then, regaining his composure, he called the faithful present to come to the altar to see what the Lord had caused to happen.

"The changed substances were not consumed. The bread-turned-Flesh and the wine-turned-Blood... were...placed in a precious ivory container. In 1713 they were enshrined in an artistic silver monstrance in which they are preserved even to the present day in the Church of St. Francis in Lanciano. Many years later, the Church, wanting to ascertain the true nature of the substances, requested modern scientists to examine them and give their verdict. In November of 1970 a team of medical experts was convened to begin the investigation. It was chaired by Professor Odoardo

Linoli. At the start of the investigation he was very skeptical of the matter, but by the middle of December he sent his first message to the Director of the Shrine. It was a very brief but dramatic telegram: 'In the beginning was the Word. And the Word was made flesh.' " 5

A friend who recently saw this host of Lanciano said it was the highlight of her trip to Europe.

Ella's Story

Ella was born in the Middle East of Jewish parents. Her home was much like those described in the Bible: the upper room was her bedroom; the room under the kitchen was where they kept their animals for the night; the well for drinking water was in the middle of the village. They had no electricity and had to weave their cotton to make material for clothes. Their shoes were made from the skins of animals.

Ella was an unwanted, unloved and molested child, afraid of everything and everybody. Only the power of God could transform her into the beautiful, strong, secure person she is today. Allow the Lord to build Your faith in His loving, healing presence as you read her moving testimony.

"Mother had three abortions after I was born. I was constantly reminded that I should have been aborted too, but something went wrong and I was born. In our home were three big bottles filled with mentholated spirits and inside the bottles were the three aborted babies at different stages of growth. They were there as a show. Whenever I did anything wrong I was quickly told that I, too, might finish up in one of those bottles like my brothers and sisters.

"I had four abortions before I was married; had a nervous breakdown at 18; and became addicted to drugs and alcohol in my twenties. I attempted suicide seven times, unable to understand why I had to live a life without meaning. My husband, chosen by my parents, was an atheist.

"Once a Catholic priest taught me two lines of prayer that turned my life around: 'Jesus, may all that is You, flow into me. May Your Body and Blood be my food and drink.' After my priest friend died, I was befriended by a Protestant pastor who taught me a love for the Bible. Although I was baptized a Christian in his church, I was not satisfied. This denomination did not really believe, 'May Your Body and Blood be my food and drink,' so I kept looking.

"Meanwhile, I was diagnosed with leukemia. This was in addition to diabetes that I had for 20 years. I knew the key to my healing was finding a place where I could receive the real Body and Blood of Jesus. Something inside kept telling me that if I could receive the Body and Blood of Jesus I would be healed.

"I found it in a Catholic church during my first healing Mass, which I attended with a friend. At the consecration I saw a vision of a lamb slain on the altar. It was the Lamb of God. I knew then that this was where I would find the Body and Blood of Jesus, and that it would bring me healing. I was received into the Catholic Church in May 1985.

"When I met Father DeGrandis in 1985 he told me I needed to forgive my father for some ways he hurt me as a child. I began a regular program of saying the *Forgiveness Prayer*. On his retreat I was healed of diabetes and the leukemia went into remission.

"I thank God for my second chance. I especially thank the Lord for allowing me to receive Him in the Eucharist. " '...Take this,' he said; 'this is My Body...' " (Mk 14:22).

> *Lord, I am not worthy to receive You, but only*
> *say the word and I shall be healed.*
> *The Body of Christ...Amen.*

"...Jesus said to them: 'Let me solemnly assure you, if you do not eat the flesh of the Son of Man and drink His Blood, you have no life in you. He who feeds on my flesh and drinks my blood has life eternal and I will raise him up on the last day' " (Jn 6:53- 54).

I think most people would probably like to live forever. On the trees in the park we can often see a heart carved with the initials of a boy and girl. Often it will read, "I love you FOREVER." Eternity is a desire of the human heart. Parents want to keep the love and presence of their children forever. We desire everlasting life because God has placed that drive in our hearts. It is the urge of self-preservation.

Jesus fulfills this desire by saying we will never die "spiritually" but can live with Him and the Father forever. This is the most consoling thought at every Christian funeral. I always preach on this scripture at that time.

People are now talking about freezing their bodies when they die so that they can be resurrected in the future by scientists with new technology. While I have doubts about this, the case is clear—they want life to continue without end.

A Eucharistic Minister's Testimony

As a priest offering Holy Mass, from time to time I get a glimpse of the reality of Jesus in the Eucharist, and it is staggering. Many priests have this experience. Listen to one eucharistic minister who also had that awareness:

"Standing in front of the congregation holding the wine cup was not a difficult job, nor did it make me nervous. However, as I held the cup during communion at one Saturday evening Mass, I was given an insight as to what it contained. That little glass cup held the Blood of Jesus Christ. Not wine and water, but the same Blood that dripped from Jesus' wounds and crown of thorns some 2,000 years ago. Although it has a different form now, it is, to Catholics, the same Blood that fell from His back after the scourging at the pillar. These few ounces in the small cup also stained the wood of the Cross. The humanity of Jesus became strikingly apparent to me as I stood looking down into the cup.

"I had a true sense of awe as I realized that this is the same blood shared by our Christian ancestors while they hid in the catacombs in Rome; the same blood which all the Popes have raised in offering to God.

"Now, every time I hold the cup, I firmly understand that this is Jesus' Blood. I still feel no sense of worthiness or unworthiness, but I do sense the value and actuality of what is in that cup."

Expectation

As you come to Holy Communion, expect the Lord to minister to you. Expect the Lord to heal you. "...you have believed, so let this be done for you" (Mt 8:13, JB). As you come to the altar to receive Jesus, accept Him as your Lord and savior. He is Lord of the problem that is burdening you right now. What is the greatest problem in your life now? What is ruining your peace of mind? What is upsetting you? Agitating you? Your children? Your health? Your unbelief? An area of living? A compulsion that you can't control? Is it finances? What is it? Bring it to the Lord. "If only I can touch his cloak...I shall get well" (Mt 9:21). Jesus tells us that we don't have to touch just the hem of his cloak—He says, "Take me! Take all of me! This is MY Body. This is MY Blood!"

Jesus is totally present under the appearance of bread, and totally present under the appearance of wine. Referring back to the story in Chapter 3, when Father Richard Woldum gave the dying boy, Johnny, the Precious Blood with an eye dropper, he was receiving the fullness of Jesus Christ.

When we make an "altar call" and come to receive the whole Jesus, we are contacting the Creator of the world, the Redeemer, the Eternal God before whom we shall stand one day. Incredible! Do we realize what we are doing when we respond to the call to eat the flesh of the Son of man and drink His Blood? This is the most precious time of the 168 hours in the week. We stand blended with the Everlasting Father in Jesus Christ. "If you only recognized God's gift..." (Jn 4:10).

In a private revelation to a priest, Jesus was heard to say: "My dear one, I am now within you. It is in the Eucharist that I am consecrated to you and you to Me. Many of My people do not realize what it means to receive My Body. My people do not realize the power they receive when they receive the Eucharist. It is My power...the power of Christ! I, in you, shall grant your heart's desire. It is I, through Eucharist, who makes your image one in the likeness of God, because you are receiving My Body. I grant you special graces, not by human desire, but by Mine. You become people of God. All you need to do is ask. My people need to be open to this." 6

As you read the sixth chapter of John, ask the Holy Spirit to teach you the stupendous truth that Jesus does indeed come with His Body and Blood to nourish, strengthen and heal you so that you can live forever.

Many people who have apparently died and had after-life experiences narrate how they did not want to return to earth after seeing the beauty of the "light" of the other world. This surpasses everything else! The closest we come to that is the marvelous, awesome presence of Jesus in the Eucharist during reception of Holy Communion. He comes to heal us physically, spiritually, emotionally and psychologically. He assures us that He wants us to rise and live with Him forever.

When you walk forward to receive communion, picture Jesus handing you the host. Don't see the eucharistic minister. See Jesus. Say to the Lord, "May your body and blood be my food and drink."

After Communion

Close your eyes and focus on Jesus. Visualize Jesus standing at the altar. See light coming from the hands of Jesus into your heart—touching you right now, healing areas of hurt or need. Surrender, lose yourself in His permeating inner presence. "...the life I live now is not my own; Christ is living in me..." (Gal 2:20).

Believe with me that the healing power emanating from Jesus is touching us, setting us free from guilt, doubt, self-hatred, self-condemnation. Believe that He is doing a deep healing of the inner self and restoring self-esteem, self-love, self-acceptance. Thank You, Lord, because we believe it is being done to us according to our faith.

Communion Reflection

For a silent communion reflection you might want to use *The Staircase of Life Prayer.* In this prayer we walk up an imaginary staircase with Jesus and Mary, each step representing a year of life. Ask Jesus to supply the paternal/male love that is needed and not received, especially from primary relationships. Ask Mary to supply the maternal/female love needed and not received, especially from primary relationships.

God is love, and He wants to heal us more than we want to be healed. It is not a matter of being worthy. It's true, we aren't worthy, but that has nothing to do with the story.

We say, "Lord, if You want to You can heal me." He says, "I do want to. Be healed!" We must be aware that we can be healed, which we can do if we get beyond our feelings of unworthiness and accept ourselves. We feel unworthy, but His love overwhelms us. He wants to cut through feelings of unworthiness, guilt, fear, resentment, bitterness, hatred, self-condemnation, lack of self-love—all the things that hold us back from truly embracing God as loving Father. He will cut through all that and release living water from our spirits. The Lord wants us to recognize that we are in need of healing; He wants us to be aware that we can be healed; He wants us to accept His healing.

This *Staircase of Life Prayer* is very simple, but powerful. It is built on the belief that prayer works; that if we ask, we are going to receive. Eventually, sometime or somewhere, we will enter into a deeper sense of God's love. During communion let us focus, through silent prayer, on His healing love. Some traumas are mentioned in each year to awaken any memories of hurts that have been buried.

Staircase of Life Prayer

Jesus and Mary, we ask for the gift of visualization, enabling us to picture ourselves walking with You up this staircase. Heal the hurts and pains of each year, filling in the gaps between the love we needed and the love we received.

I see myself born as a little infant into Your hands. Take me, Jesus, and walk me through the first year of life. Touch, heal and make whole.

Come into the second year of life and heal the traumas, especially rejections by any other children in the family.

Lord I see You carrying me through the third year, healing the hurts and pains and filling me with the love I needed.

Through the fourth year I thank You, Lord, for healing the hurts, pains and fears of life, especially those associated with my family.

Take me gently through the fifth year, Lord. Thank You for walking with me through the first five years of my life.

In the sixth year, Lord, let me experience healing, peace, joy, love and life because of Your healing touch.

Heal all the hurts of the seventh year, Lord: pains of going to school, a new teacher, strange children, the trauma of studies, and fears associated with moving.

Take me gently into the eighth year. Thank you for carrying me lovingly through this year. Mary, supply a mother's love that was needed at this time, perhaps because my mother was sick or in the hospital. Please make up for any deprivation in the eighth year.

Lord, supply love in the ninth year; especially supply the affection from my father that I needed and did not receive. Thank you, Lord.

Thank You for the healings in the tenth year of my life. Heal any anger I had toward my parents. Touch that anger and give me a sense of security, knowing that I am loved. Thank You, Lord, for healing the first ten years of my life.

In the 11th year, Lord, I became self-conscious about my appearance. Touch, heal and make whole.

Thank You for healing the 12th year. Set me free from all the fear and guilt, especially sexual guilt. Thank You, Jesus.

Take me into the 13th year, Lord. Set me free from the self-consciousness I felt for being a teenager.

Jesus, I picture You and Mary walking with me in the 14th year. Mary, supply large doses of a mother's love. Give me a sense of being loved, esteemed and valued.

Touch me gently in the 15th year. Lord, give me a sense of security in this year amidst all my insecurities. Thank You, Lord, for the healings of the first fifteen years of my life.

Touch me now in the 16th year, Lord. Heal this difficult period.

Take me gently into the 17th year, especially times when I hated everything about myself. Give me a sense of love and acceptance.

Into the 18th and 19th years, touch and make whole. Heal all the traumas of late teenage years, especially in the area of sexual guilt.

Lord, touch me deeply in the 20th year when I was rejected by people of the opposite sex. Touch me and set me free. Take me through the years of the twenties, touching and healing the hurts and pains of interpersonal relationships.

Lord, I see You taking me into the 21st year, supplying all my needs.

Thank You for being there in the 22nd year, healing tensions associated with marital partners, in-laws and other family members. Touch and make whole.

In the 23rd year, Lord, heal all the traumas of trying to adjust to marriage. Touch all the mis-understandings and anger that come from this adjustment.

Into the 24th and 25th years, heal any frustrations and feelings of abandonment, perhaps because of illness. Set me free and fill me with Your Spirit. Thank You, Lord, for touching the first twenty-five years.

Touch the 26th year, especially any pain associated with death of someone close: grandmother, father, mother, sister, child, friend, neighbor. Heal the traumas of death and set me free from fear of death.

In the 27th and 28th years, touch me deeply as I adjust to single living. Let Your Spirit flow through me.

In the 29th year, heal all the feelings of rejection, misunderstandings, false accusations. Touch me deeply and heal me, Lord.

Fill me with Your Spirit in the 30th year. Thank You, Lord, for healing the first thirty years of my life.

In the thirties, Lord, touch the 31st, 32nd and 33rd years. Heal all the anxieties and fears—all the care and concern about the children and anxieties of work.

In the 34th year, Lord, please touch problems of drinking in the family. Heal the trauma of difficult decisions.

Jesus and Mary, take me into the 35th and 36th years of my life. Touch and heal any arguments with neighbors.

Into the 37th and 38th years, touch all the fears associated with job loss, financial responsibilities and growing older.

Touch the 39th and 40th years, Lord. Thank You for touching the first forty years of my life. Mary, my mother, give me that sense of closeness, warmth and love.

Lord, touch all the turmoil and change in the 41st and 42nd years.

Touch the traumas of mid-life crisis in the 43rd and 44th years: children leaving home; rejection by a spouse. Touch and heal, Lord.

In the 45th year, Lord, heal the feelings of failure, feelings that I have not achieved professionally. Also touch the feelings of not having achieved as a Christian and the temptations of faith. Lord, touch, heal and make whole.

Into the 46th year, touch the traumas of children leaving home and marital discord.

In the 47th year, touch any anxiety over grandchildren.

Take me gently through the 48th and 49th years, Lord.

Touch the 50th year, Lord. Heal the first fifty years of life. Set me free and fill me with Your Spirit.

Touch, heal and make whole the 51st year, Lord.

In the 52nd, 53rd, 54th and 55th years, Lord, let Your Spirit move. Touch all those deep fears, especially fears of death.

In the 56th and 57th years touch fears of sickness and loneliness.

Touch the fears of the 58th year: family moving away, loss of marriage partner. Touch and heal those traumas, Lord.

In the 59th year, touch the pain of being out of touch with my children. Heal that hurt, Lord.

Touch the 60th year, Lord. Heal the first 60 years of my life.

In the 61st year, heal the feeling of being unwanted, not needed, unappreciated and not understood.

Lord, take me gently into the 62nd, 63rd and 64th year and heal the fear of approaching retirement.

In the 65th year, Lord, heal the trauma of seeing death in my family.

Lord Jesus, take me gently through the sixties and into the seventies. Let Your healing love flow through these years, and into the eighties. Lord, touch me powerfully in the eighties, as I prepare for my heavenly homecoming. Complete all the unfinished business in my life. Let me look back through my life with eyes of forgiveness and eyes of love. Let Your love, healing, and forgiveness permeate every moment of my life. Thank You, Lord, for all the healings of my life.

JoAnn's Story

JoAnn Miller of Milwaukee, Wisconsin compares inner healing prayer with peeling an onion, layer by layer, and reminds us that we need to let God's love touch every area of our lives. She reflects, "He knows all about us. He knows the things that can destroy or paralyze our minds and bodies and hold us captives of the past." In the following testimony she shares about a healing she received when I was doing a healing meditation after communion.

"The priest said we should ask God to reveal to us an area in our lives that still needed healing. We prayed a while, and then we were silent, letting the Holy Spirit enlighten us about a particular area. My thoughts flew to a damp, dark musty basement on the farm where I lived with my grandmother and brothers. When I was very young (age 3 or 4) I was locked in that dark, damp basement as punishment. For years since then I didn't like closed doors and musty smells made me ill. Even now, 46 years later, I can still remember how that basement looked. There was a big cistern in a corner, and a root cellar. In my little mind I was always afraid of being put in the cistern and drowning. I have hated basements all my life.

"The priest then said, 'Ask Jesus to come with you.' So in my imagination Jesus and I walked to the basement and He opened the heavy cellar doors. Light flooded the steps. Every place He walked, His healing light flooded the area. Even the cistern was transformed. The thing that smelled with its stale water became a thing of beauty when Jesus walked past, and there was fresh sparkling water in it. He touched every area of the room and it became new. Even the musty dirt floor became beautiful and fragrant. As Jesus walked across the floor, flowers of every color sprang forth. It was breathtaking.

"My prison was now a thing of beauty, healed with God's love. He also enabled me to forgive the person who had put me there. I am free!"

Testimonies from Survey Respondents

* A friend received communion for her husband, having such a strong belief in the power of "two shall be made one." I was overwhelmed by her faith. It opened a new and lasting source of growth for me. This in turn led me to share and pass on what she witnessed to me. Since then I have heard of much healing from my family by receiving communion on behalf of others. (anonymous)

* My severe migraine headache was gone after the Body and Blood were elevated during a healing Mass. There were lights all over my head. I could not explain what I saw, but the pain was gone. (Ann Belale)

* During communion on a silent retreat I received the baptism of the Holy Spirit, but didn't realize it until weeks later. I experienced a total cleansing, overwhelming love, peace and forgiveness. My spiritual life changed dramatically, as did the rest of my life. I always knew as a child that Jesus was with me. I always felt He took care of me and had something special for me. As an adult, on that silent retreat, I discovered that it was really true. (Sue Cevasco)

* After the ending of a relationship that was quite painful to break off, my Lord came to me after communion as if with a surgeon's hand. He entered my heart and scraped it out as if cleansing the woundedness. I cried because it hurt emotionally, but felt uplifted afterwards. (Jerilyn Gravois)

* A man I knew in the Philippines despaired of ever experiencing social justice in that country. This was a number of years ago when the country was on the verge of political and economic collapse. The man joined a left-leaning communist movement poised to

destabilize the government by killing prominent leaders of the community, local government and the Church. On the eve of his departure he went to his final Mass and gave God His last chance, asking Him to prove He existed. During communion as he received the Eucharist, grace struck him in a violent way and he fell to the floor. He went through an instant conversion. He tells me what probably saved him was a seed of faith planted when he was in the seminary years ago. Today he is a lay evangelist dedicated to working for the Church. (Patsy Gonzales)

* I came to Mass sad and lonely, heavy hearted, expecting nothing. I was not at peace with myself because of certain relationships. Just before communion I felt Jesus' presence lifting my burdens and putting love and peace in my heart. I cried. I will never forget that moment. (Helen)

* I was brought to the Mass at the Colegio de San Agustin in Makati in October 1988 by a pediatrician friend of my father because I had been suffering from blood in the urine for four years. None of the tests to determine kidney or urinary disorders revealed the source of the problem. During the Mass you mentioned that kidneys were being healed and said that those being healed would feel something like a warm hand on their backs. I felt it, but thought it was because I had been sitting for some time. Exactly one week later I woke up without a trace of blood in my urine. When I told my father, he said, 'The moment you got into the car to go to the Mass I knew you would be healed.' It has remained clear for two months. The doctor wants to monitor my system for another year to be certain. (Maria Luz F. Paje, the Philippines)

* The love of God manifested in me in a healing Mass at Colegio de San Agustin on October 23, 1988. Through *The Forgiveness Prayer* I came to realize that I have been very hard on myself and unable to

forgive myself. I prayed that all blocks that hinder my spiritual growth be removed. I found myself ready to forgive those who hurt me and able to ask forgiveness of those I hurt. During the Mass, just before the final blessing, the Lord healed a pain in my elbow that was caused by a fall almost a year ago. I had slipped, and to avoid banging my head to the wall, I used my right hand as support to cushion the impact of my fall. During Mass I felt heaviness in my right hand up to the elbow. I could not raise it. A force quite strong pulled my hand and rotated my arm. I felt my right arm being detached from my shoulder joint and then, like a spring or magnet, it went back to the shoulder joint and the pain suddenly disappeared. I heard a 'click' sound as my arm attached to the shoulder joint. Since then my friends call me Joy. Praise the Lord. (Rowena L. Gonzales, Manila, the Philippines)

* After two years of dieting, medication and doctor consultations for high cholesterol (measured at 350) I have been cleansed! The doctors had been warning me of the extremely high risk—so high one doctor said I wouldn't 'last' without a stroke or heart attack until my next appointment. On February 23, 1990 I attended a Mass at St. Margaret Mary Church in Slidell, LA. During the Mass a word was given that someone was being healed through cleansing of the blood. I felt a warm thrust in my veins and through my heart. When the results of my laboratory tests were given to me, my cholesterol registered at an acceptable 275. I knew that God had healed me. (Betty Strasser)

* I was suffering with pain in my hip all during the weekend conference. In spite of the prayers during the weekend, by Mass on Sunday I was experiencing the worst pain of the weekend. During Mass I had a talk with the Lord about that severe pain. When I received communion I had no pain. I returned to my chair and felt a 'readjustment' or a change in my hip socket, and another 'readjustment' or movement

across my hip/abdomen. My leg then felt very light as if it would float straight up. Several days have now gone by since that experience and I have not had any more of that same pain. Praise the Lord for His healing and tenderness. (Rita Pilger)

* I celebrated a healing Mass for the people of Naga in the chapel of the Carmelite Monastery on a Saturday morning. I did not know the condition of any of the people at the Mass as no one had asked me to pray for any special intention. I stressed the importance of forgiveness, led them in *The Forgiveness Prayer*, and gave everyone general absolution. During the homily I was led to tell the people to look up during the elevation of the Body and Blood of Christ. 'As you are looking at the Lord Jesus and adoring Him in faith,' I said, 'pray for healing. Especially if you pray for others,' I added, 'you will be healed.'

One woman, Nena Bichara, took my words as gospel truth. She had been suffering from a goiter for three years. The doctors could do nothing about it except to recommend surgery that, of course, she did not want to undergo. During the elevation of the Body of Christ she prayed for different people. Then she added, 'and also, Lord, do not forget my goiter.' At once she felt a power hit her. She knew instantly that she was healed. She nudged her son next to her and said, 'I am healed.' He answered, 'Be quiet, mommy. People will think you are crazy.' After the Mass she called her doctor and insisted on an examination. He told her to come next week as it was already Saturday afternoon, but, like the persistent widow in the gospel, she got her way. The doctor could find no trace of the goiter! Three months later in Manila she went to another doctor who did not know her case. She asked for a complete examination and asked the doctor to be sure to check for goiters. The doctor told her, 'You do not have any sign of a goiter. You have never had one.' Praise God!

There was also a woman in the music ministry in Guam who was instantly healed of sweaty hands as she lifted them in praise!" (From a letter from Father Arnold "Arnie" Boehme, OCD, in the Philippines)

Healing Reflections

* Reflect on how much attention would be given to the president of the United States if he were to come to your home.

* Imagine the Pope visiting your home.

* Think about the intense focus of attention on his person as he entered your home.

* One greater than the Pope comes to you in the Eucharist!

PART V

CONCLUDING RITE

Concluding Rite

The Lord be with you.

And also with you.

*May almighty God bless you, the Father, and the
Son, and the Holy Spirit.*

What does "blessing" mean to you? Some definitions of
blessing include: "To invoke divine care for; to confer
prosperity or happiness upon; to dedicate; to approve;
to endorse." As we reflect upon God's covenant of
blessing through Abraham and into the New
Covenant, we see that God has made tremendous
provision for blessing His people.

We all need to experience blessing. We need
continually to receive it from our Heavenly Father,
and we need to be givers of blessings to others. We need
to know that we are deeply valued, that we are
important. We need to communicate to others that
they have high value.

Consider the scars of the unblessed in our society.
Consider the abandoned, the outcast, the homeless, the
unloved. Reflect on the destructive behavior of those
who run here and there searching for acceptance,
longing for a blessing but experiencing curses instead.

Through the Mass we can enter into the life of
Jesus in a powerful way, and experience the curses in
our lives being changed to blessings (Deut 23:5). The
Lord says in Joel 2:25, "...I will repay you for the years
which the locust has eaten, the grasshopper, the

devourer, and the cutter..." The blessing goes deeper into the layers of pain in our lives the more we place ourselves in the presence of the One who blesses. He is a God of restoration, a God of blessing.

Each part of the Mass aids in the healing, blessing process: The Introductory Rite, the Liturgy of the Word, the Liturgy of the Eucharist, and the Concluding Rite. Enter into each part intimately, deeply and honestly. Open up and receive the full effects our Lord intends for you to receive. Go to church with great faith that the Lord wants to heal you far beyond your expectations. He wants to set you free and use you as an instrument of His healing love to set others free.

We are called to carry that blessing to others, and thus extend the ministry of Jesus. There are people alive today who should be dead, but because there was someone who knew how to pray effectively, how to bless, they are still alive. Many people have been healed of alcoholism, drug addiction, mental illness and major physical diseases because Christians prayed.

The vision of a renewed Church is achieved when people realize that God is love; He loves them unconditionally; provides for their needs; equips them; and sends them forth in His name to pray with and serve others. We are nourished and sent forth to "preach and heal." When Christians take hold of their vocation and start praying with others, renewal within the Church will increase.

In the Concluding Rite the blessing of the priest stirs up the sacrament of confirmation that mandates us to share Jesus Christ with others—by example, by praying with them and by any means the Lord suggests. As people share their stories, others will be opened to receive prayer for healing, especially spiritual healing. Indeed many today have lost faith, but are waiting for an opportunity to experience God's love and presence.

The whole thrust of evangelization is rooted in the Eucharist. I pray that the Lord will continue to unfold in our hearts an understanding of the great gift of the Eucharist. I pray that the wonder of this great gift will rise in our spirits and bring great faith in the healing power of the Mass.

Lord Jesus, we thank You that You have called us by name; You called us to Mass to heal us, to liberate us, to set us free. You called us to empower us to heal broken hearts. Lord, let our healing be so deep that we walk out of Mass new creations, new people, healed in body, mind and spirit. Thank You, Heavenly Father, for loving us so much. Thank You, Jesus, for not bearing to leave us, and thus sending the Holy Spirit. Thank You, Holy Spirit, for guiding us into the freedom of children of God. In the name of the Father, and of the Son, and of the Holy Spirit. Amen.

The Mass is ended.
Go in peace to love and serve the Lord.

Thanks be to God.

Coming Home

Father Ken Roberts in an article in *New Covenant*, talks about loving people back into the Church. He says, "A lot of people leave because of misconceptions about the sacraments and church teachings....some leave because they have been hurt." When asked the question, "What brings these people back?" he responded, "I've met many people who left and came back because they had a greater appreciation of the Eucharist after they'd been away from it for a while. I met some people at a big charismatic gathering who were witnessing about their return to the Catholic Church after a three-year absence. They eventually found that there was something missing—the Eucharist and the other sacraments." He continues, "Unconditional love is the only way to win back those who have already left the Church. I met a young man from San Diego who had left the church and was trying to convert Catholics because he was convinced that the Catholic Church is the Antichrist. I said to him, 'Son, I'm not going to argue religion with you. I'll tell you what I believe, and I'll tell you why I believe it. But I'll love you whether you believe it or not, because that is what Jesus told me to do.' He began to cry, and was then opened by the Spirit to want to come back to the Church. Treating people with unconditional love is the only way to draw back those who have left the Church." [1]

A question was asked in the survey, "What would you say to non-practicing Catholics to encourage them to return to Mass?" Some representative responses are included below.

Encouragements from Survey Respondents

* I returned to the Church after more than 17 years, and now receive communion again. Now God lets me know through my tears that He hears my prayers and everything will be okay. I feel His presence with me at Mass. There is immense value and grace received at Mass. (Dolores Gorospe)

* I had been away from the Church for thirty years. After returning I went to my first healing Mass. It was a small group, about 40 people, and we were invited to stand around the altar. I really felt a part of that celebration for the first time in my life. I couldn't stop crying, it was such a beautiful and healing experience. (Peggy Hurtado)

* I was out of the Church for six years. I was married outside the Church and the Church closed the doors on me and my children. Through a Mass with Father DeGrandis on a retreat I was released and set free from those hurts. That week I was accepted back into the Church and my walk with the Lord started a totally new life for me. (Marisol Cesar)

* If you develop a personal relationship with Him you can receive love, peace, forgiveness and healing— more than you ever thought possible in the Catholic Church. (Sue Cevasco)

* Jesus is really present—come and open up to this experience. (Eileen)

* God loves you. He wants you to be happy. He wants to heal you. (Marcellino Salazar)

* My physical healings have been at Mass. (Christine Stewart)

* You will feel a warmth and serenity never felt before if you ask. (Mary Moore)

* Jesus healed me at Mass. (Irma Lasley)

* Be open for the Lord to touch you and welcome you back. Relax about everything. Look around for a spiritual family that speaks to your heart. (Traudel Weibel)

* Jesus loves you just the way you are. Come home. (Raymond Means, Jr.)

Joanne Winchester's Story

Joanne Winchester shares about her return to the Church in the following story.

"Dad was in the Air Force and, among other places, we lived in France and California. Those two locales provided a wealth of shrines for a devout Catholic family to visit. In California we toured all the Spanish missions, except one. We never made it to the Mission San Juan Capistrano, famous for the swallows that returned from their southern migration each year on the Feast of St. Joseph. I was always fascinated by this event and promised myself that someday I would see it.

"When I married a non-Catholic I gradually quit attending Mass and receiving the sacraments. After some years, we were divorced and I returned to work to support myself and our son. I remained away from the Church throughout these years.

"When my employer asked me to take an assignment in California, I accepted, leaving behind friends, family, and home in Virginia. My five-year-old son and I set up residence near the office, which happened to be five miles from the Mission San Juan Capistrano.

"One Sunday I decided to make the long overdue visit to the missed shrine of my childhood. Walking about the beautiful grounds, my son and I came upon the chapel and I saw that a Mass was to begin in ten minutes. I figured those few minutes would be enough time to view the chapel's interior before Mass started.

"As we entered the vestibule, an usher stopped me to ask if my son and I would take the gifts up at the Offertory. I explained that I had not been to Mass in years and just wanted to see the chapel. He invited us to stay. His look and his voice were so soothing that I found myself saying yes. He then reinvited us to present the gifts. My protests that I would not know how or when to do so were met by the same warm smile and an assurance that he would guide me. I weakly agreed and we followed him to the first pew to wait for Mass to start.

"This kind gentleman assisted at Mass and did indeed cue me for the Offertory. After delivering the gifts, we returned to our pew and soon reached the singing of *The Our Father.* As my son and I stood with our hands joined and I began to sing the beautiful words, I was overcome with a longing for the inner peace of Christ. I knew then that, like the faithful swallows of Capistrano, I had come home again." [2]

Barbara Olsen's Story

Barbara Olsen of Escondido, California, left the Church when she married and didn't go to Mass for 13 years. Her decision to return to the Church was an important part of her healing. As you read the gripping story of abuse, loss, and deep emotional pain, think about the areas in your life that need the miracle touch of the Eucharistic Lord. As you reflect upon her journey home into the arms of her loving Heavenly Father, consider again your relationship with God the Father. He is here to bless you even now.

"When I was a little girl of eight my father's body was found floating down a river. I had always felt deep inside that I was responsible for his death, but I couldn't remember why. I never asked any questions; we never talked about him or his death. Only once, more than twenty years later, did I question my mother. My inquiry bothered her a great deal. She asked, 'Don't you remember the fights we used to have? The police had to come and break them apart.' I replied, 'No, I don't remember.' She asked, 'Don't you remember that he abused you and I had to kick him out of the house?' I replied again, 'No, I don't remember.' In an angry conversation with my brother he asked me, 'Don't you remember that mom was investigated for dad's death because of you?' I responded once more, 'No, I don't remember.'

"His death was tragic for me. Though the children were told that he committed suicide, I always felt that two of my uncles had killed him because of me, although I couldn't remember why. It wasn't until after both men had died that I asked my mother why I had that feeling. She said it wasn't true; nothing else was said and it was laid to rest again.

"All my life I had felt guilty, and never knew why. I broke away from the Church when I married and didn't go to Mass for 13 years. Reincarnation, astrology and New Age practices became a part of my life.

"I also had an abortion, unaware of the deep emotional pain this would trigger. Night after night, for weeks and months and years, my pillow was soaked with tears of shame and sorrow. But I didn't yet know that I needed Jesus.

"It was the loving attention of a friend that brought me to a turning point. Through her persistence I started going to a Bible study in Southern California. Reading the Word of God changed my life. I began to see my emptiness and my need for Jesus. My decision to return to the Catholic Church was an important part of the healing. Confession was difficult, but I was met with gentleness and forgiveness.

"When I later yielded to the Holy Spirit at a deeper level, the presence of the Lord was so powerful that I cried and hid my face; I was so ashamed of my sin. Then I felt the words, 'Be not ashamed,' being written on my heart. I saw between God and me a veil of blood, and knew through this vision that God does not see me as I am, but through a veil of the Blood of Jesus. I was filled with incredible joy and felt His powerful love for me.

"I was not aware that I was still carrying a lot of deeply buried guilt until sometime later on a retreat when a priest told me that Jesus wanted to heal me of a burden. Sometimes I would tell myself that I must have misunderstood my mother. Surely she did not mean sexual abuse. My father would not have done that to me.

"After I told the story to the priest and a prayer leader, when they were praying for me, the woman saw in a vision the Holy Family surrounding me. Jesus assumed the role of my father, and He delighted in me.

"During a Mass for my father, I was able to forgive him for not being the father I needed; for hurting me; for dying and leaving me. This was the greatest hurt. The abuse brought me guilt; his death stopped my love.

"After the Mass my mother and I were able to talk about the abuse and the death. Much later I read that many women who choose abortion have unresolved grief over the death of a loved one, and many have been abused as children.

"It became clear in time that I had been deeply fearful of Father God and uncertain of His love. I couldn't go to Him myself; I was too afraid. I didn't realize that 'father' and 'Father' were so closely bound. Jesus stepped in and bridged the gap for both of them, so that I might forgive one and loose the bonds of sin, and know the everlasting love of the other. When Jesus took my father's place, I was able to open up and receive the love of Father God.

"Jesus and my Heavenly Father are helping me to recognize the love of my earthly father, too. Way down deep I felt he never loved me; they are showing me that this is not true.

"I pray for those who need a miracle in their father relationships to turn to the Lord Jesus for help. I pray for those who carry a heavy burden, who feel guilty for a tragedy in their lives, who cry themselves to sleep over past sins, and who have wounds that are so deep that they are not consciously aware of them. I pray that you seek the Lord Jesus. He has never stopped loving us—even when we turned away from Him; even in the midst of our sins; and especially in our woundedness. He desires so much for us to be aware of His love; to heal us; to fill us with joy; to fill us with forgiveness for others and ourselves; to fill us with peace, love and joy. He desires for us to come home. He is waiting with open arms."

Healing Reflections

Have you a relative, a neighbor, a friend who has left the Church? Or is there someone you know in the hospital, in prison, or homebound who just needs a welcoming word to return home to the Catholic Church?

* Pray for them daily, especially at communion, asking the Lord to heal their hurts.

* Ask the Holy Spirit for wisdom as you reach out in love and in sharing.

* Have a Mass celebrated for them and their family, both living and dead.

Funeral Masses

Life is serious business. Many live as though they will never die and appear before Jesus Christ. One of the times that people are very open to the gospel message is during a funeral Mass. Then they are faced with their mortality and that of their loved ones. They are often ready for change. All the big issues of life are laid before them at that time. Because of this fact, I find it easy to evangelize during funeral Masses, and encourage the inclusion of the fundamental issues of the gospel in the homily.

It can be a time of celebration for deeply devout Christians, especially if unfinished business in the relationship with the deceased has been completed. Muriel Neveux, R.N., of Massachusetts commented in the survey that her greatest healing came at her mother's funeral Mass: "I had a tremendous sense of peace because I knew she was with the Lord. Everyone else was crying and I was joyful." Another respondent, Chona, said, "My father's burial Mass was the most meaningful Mass I ever experienced." A legal assistant shared about a funeral Mass for a devout Catholic, saying, "I am a music minister and have never seen a congregation so responsive and joyous. I have seen dozens of weddings that weren't as joyous as this funeral. It was the faith and hope of the congregation that made the Mass special."

Father Jeff Steffon of Los Angeles, California, has a special healing prayer for funeral Masses, which we offer below:

*"Lord, I ask Your permission to stand in the gap for _____.
Lord, I ask that You heal the way that _____ died. Heal any
confusion, fear or pain that he/she experienced in life.*

*In _____ name I forgive all those people who hurt
_____ in his/her life, whether they be living or deceased. I ask
that You, Lord, will now heal all those hurts.*

*In the name of _____ I ask forgiveness of all those whom
he/she has hurt in his/her life, whether they be living or deceased. I
ask that these people will now be healed of the hurts that they
received from him/her.*

*I ask You, Lord Jesus, to go to where _____ is and bring
him/her to the throne of light. Permit him/her to behold our
Father's face and let His light shine upon him/her. In Jesus' name I
pray. Amen.*

Healing Reflections

* Visualize your funeral Mass. How would you like it to
  be offered?

* Write an epitaph for your tombstone. For what would
  you like people to remember you?

* Select the music for your funeral Mass.

* What funeral has been the most inspiring for you?

* When you die, will you regret the time you spent in
  weekly or daily Mass?

Appendix

Survey Responses

Nineteen men and 81 women responded to the survey on healing through the Mass. All but four of the respondents considered themselves a part of the charismatic renewal.

Some of the questions and responses are included below. Others are incorporated in the book.

Mass Attendance

38 - daily
32 - weekly
30 - 2 to 5 times a week
 3 - when possible

Why do you go to Mass?

praise	worship	thanksgiving
strength	peace	community
pray	joy	guidance
solace	relationship	healing
guilt	love	hear the word
obligation	grace	transformation

On a scale of 1 to 10 (with 10 being the highest) what is your normal level of active participation in Mass?

	1	2	3	4	5	6	7	8	9	10
MEN					1	1	5	6	3	3
WOMEN	1			1	4	6	15	14	14	26

What do you recommend to improve participation in Mass?

* Pray more, pray actively, more prayer time, pray scriptures before Mass, meditate, pray before and after, pray for priest

* Don't day dream, don't drift, ignore distractions, stop looking around, don't look at others going to communion, stop mind from wandering during homily, erase busy thoughts, don't go to sleep, don't hold back, don't be shy, reach out in kiss of peace

* Feel His Spirit, place more faith in the Holy Spirit

* More devotion, more enthusiasm, more love, more praise, more forgiveness, more expectation

* Act on the message from readings, learn why each part of Mass is healing, learn what to expect, share with others about Mass, listen from heart, concentrate

Is the Mass a healing service?

	Yes	No	Maybe
MEN	17	1	1

	Yes	No	Yes with intellectual assent
WOMEN	78	1	2

What formed your belief that Mass is a healing service?

Scripture	baptism in the Holy Spirit
personal experience	hearing testimonies
literature	observing family and friends
faith in Jesus	various teachings

Do you generally expect to be healed at Mass?

26 respondents said "No," with the following reasons:

> need for personal conversion
> it is not taught or expected
> often I don't feel ready for healing
> don't know why
> lack expectant faith
> don't think about healing at Mass

74 answered "Yes," with following representative reasons:

> I believe it
> I know He loves me
> He promises miracles
> Because we need it
> He's proven it to me personally
> It's a gift of God's love
> Many personal experiences
> Because He's powerful, He's alive, He can do anything and He loves me
> His words are effective medicine
> For over 60 years I've been regularly healed at Mass

What kinds of healing have you received at Mass in the past year?

peace	togetherness	understanding
tears	love	carried through trials
divorce	heart	family relationships
cancer	headaches	unity with husband
sciatica	blood pressure	elbow
back	throat	tonsils
anxiety	depression	physical pain
rage	unforgiveness	lifting of burdens
anger	hurt feelings	resentments
fear	grief and loss	emotional scars
courage	strength to go on	

freed from drugs and alcohol
freed from fear of singing and tithing

What part of the liturgy is the most healing for you?

communion (68)	psalms	scripture
homily	penitential rite	music
offertory	praise	Our Father

What are your main prayer concerns at Mass?

spiritual problems (34)	relationships (18)
unforgiveness (6)	health (5)
alcohol problems (1)	

What kind of feeling do you experience in holy places?

peace (37)	warmth and love (12)
wonder and awe (11)	joy (9)

sense of safety, belonging, comfort, security (5)
Like I'm bathed in the noonday sun
Like I've just had a good meal when I was hungry
I feel like I can fly
I feel sanctified
Largeness of spirit

Survey of Priests

Have you ever been healed at Mass?

Yes	No	No answer
3	3	2

What type of healing did you receive?

Physical	Psychological	Spiritual
0	2	2

Describe the healing

* Psychological healing: great moments of peace, absence of fear, scent of roses and incense (Rev. Dan Wetzler)

* Spiritual healing: Realization of grace of conversion through confession of sin (Rev. Dan Wetzler)

* Each time I celebrate Mass I find the time after Holy Communion so reassuring, refreshing; a moment of recreation and healing. That time is very special to me as I receive answers, solutions to parish situations. It seems everything comes together for me at that time. (Rev. Thomas J. Flanagan)

* A deep sense of peace with healing in a broad sense of the word. (Rev. Paul Steinmetz, S.J.)

* Healing of ties to occult involvement of a family member. (Rev. Jeff Steffon)

What was your most profound experience at Mass?

* I was at Lourdes concelebrating Mass at the grotto in November 1979. During the Prayer of the Faithful I had a need to include everyone who was a part of my life and priesthood, family and friends. In that moment I just looked out in my spirit and saw every one of them. (Rev. Thomas J. Flanagan)

* At the consecration, realizing I was at the center of the world and of time. (Rev. Paul Steinmetz, S.J.)

* At my ordination Mass the Lord told me I'd experience something special. I now know that it was a form of resting in the Spirit. The whole experience was deeply moving and profound. (Father Thomas Foster, S.J.)

* During the consecration it was as if time was

suspended. When I genuflected I almost could not get back up. The presence of the Lord was so powerful I almost fell down. (Father Jeff Steffon)

* I was saying a Mass on a card table in a hall for a ladies' guild. I remembered hearing a story of a priest holding the blessed sacrament in front of each person and it inspired me to do the same at this Mass. At the elevation I slowly fanned the small group with Jesus in the sacrament. It suddenly dawned on me that I was really holding Jesus. For the first time in my 46 years of priesthood I felt that I was really holding Him. Just thinking of it brings tears to my eyes. (name withheld)

* I have been praying the family tree Mass for six years at this writing, averaging at least one a week. [1] I have seen many healings, especially of family relationships. (Rev. Mario S. Termini)

What do you consider the three main healing elements in Mass?

Gospel readings (3)   Consecration (2)
Homily   Communion (3)
Time after Communion (2)   Penitential Rite (3)

What can we, as priests, do to open people to the Mass?

* Constant reference to the healing power of the Mass both during the liturgy and individual sharing time.

* Be open ourselves. The priest must be baptized in the Holy Spirit. Believe in it ourselves. Open ourselves to a deeper affective spiritual life. Be men of the Spirit. This witness will attract people to the Mass and life in the Spirit. Be role models.

* Work toward freedom of Spirit to move within the structure as well as outside the Mass structure.

* Prepare for Mass. Say Mass devoutly, with meaning. Put as much feeling as possible in the Mass. Try to help the congregation understand that God is present and we (the priests) are talking to God. Explain it more frequently. Say Mass with small groups, at a table.

* Teach them how to pray the Mass for healing!

* Share our own faith.

What three areas would you like emphasized in this book?

Introduction	Collect
Our Father	Forgiveness
Sign of Peace	Receiving the Eucharist

* Have people pray over each other during the Prayer of the Faithful. In my experience 90% of the people like this prayer. (Fr. Jeff Steffon)

* Tell them that Christ comes in four ways: Assembly, Word, Sacrament and Ministers. (Rev. Albin Gietzen)

* That we the priests must come with forgiving hearts.

* All the areas work together to make God present.

* The time when we accept Christ as our Lord and Savior.

* Dismissal

* Never to pass up a moment to receive the Eucharist.

Notes

Preface

1. Austin Flannery, O.P., *Vatican Collection.* Volume 1: *Vatican II, The Conciliar and Post Conciliar Documents.* (Northport, New York: Costello Publishing Company, Inc., 1975), p. 16.

2. Theodore E. Dobson, *Say But The Word* (Ramsey, New Jersey: Paulist Press, 1984), p. 4.

3. Barbara Shlemon, R.N., "The Healing Power of the Eucharist," leaflet from Our Lady of Divine Providence, 702 Bayview Avenue, Clearwater, Florida.

Chapter 2

1. Michael D. Guinan, O.F.M.. *Covenant in the Old Testament* (Chicago, IL: Franciscan Herald Press, 1975), p.8.

2. "Dogmatic Constitution on Divine Revelation," *Documents of Vatican II*, Chapter 4, paragraph 14.

Chapter 3

1. Morton Kelsey, *Psychology, Medicine and Christian Healing* (New York, NY: Harper and Row, 1988), p. 99.

Chapter 4

1.   *The Church's Confession of Faith*, translated by Stephen Wentworth Arndt (San Francisco, CA: Ignatius Press, 1987), p. 206.

2.   Ibid, p. 58.

3.   Condensed from "God is my Father" by Doris Deutch, *New Covenant*, June 1986, p. 18-19.

4.   *The Church's Confession of Faith*, p. 186-187.

Chapter 5

1.   I recommend my books *To Forgive is Divine*, *Forgiveness and Inner Healing* (with Betty Tapscott) and *Healing the Broken Heart*. Available from HOM Books, 108 Aberdeen St., Lowell, MA 01850.

Chapter 6

1.   *Diary of Sister Faustina* (Stockbridge, MA: Marian Helpers, 1987), #1775.

2.   *I am Your Jesus of Mercy*, (Milford, OH: The Riehle Foundation, P.O. Box 7, Milford, OH, 1989), p.12.

Chapter 7

1.   Father Chris Aridas, "Fostering Praise in a Prayer Meeting," Dove Leaflet #19, Benedictine Abbey, Pecos, NM 87552.

Chapter 8

1.   It is recommended to deepen one's whole approach to the Mass that a daily holy hour be made.   For help we recommend the booklet

Miracle Hour: A Method of Prayer That Will Change Your Life, by Linda Schubert, P.O. Box 4034, Santa Clara, CA 95056 ($3.00 shipping included).

2.   Bettie Welch, "An Atheist who found God in Paris," *The Messenger*, Covington, KY.

Chapter 9

1.   "Dogmatic Constitution on Divine Revelation," *Documents of Vatican II*, Chapter 6, paragraph 26.

2.   Ibid, chapter 3, Paragraph 11.

3.   *I am Your Jesus of Mercy*, p. 12.

4.   Dorothea DeGrandis Sudol, *The Healing Jesus in Scripture*, 108 Aberdeen St., Lowell, MA 01850, pp. 5-7.

5.   Rene Laurentin, *Miracles in El Paso?* (Ann Arbor, MI: Servant Publications, 1982), pp. 104-105.

Chapter 10

1.   "Constitution on the Sacred Liturgy," *Documents of Vatican II*, Chapter 2, Paragraph 52.

Chapter 12

1.   Flannery, *Vatican Collection*, p. 18.

2.   Rev. Gerald P. Ruane, Ph.D., *The Greatest Healing Gifts*—Volume 1, The Eucharist (Caldwell, NJ: Sacred Heart Press, 1989), pp. 7-8.

3.   Father Luke Zimmer, Apostolate of Christian Renewal, 411 First Street, Fillmore, CA 93015.

Chapter 13

1.   "Constitution on the Sacred Liturgy," *Documents of Vatican II,* Chapter 1, Paragraph 10.

Chapter 14

1.   George A. Maloney, S.J., "Healing the Sick: How can a Pastor Respond?" Part II, *Crux,* February 1979.

2.   Walter J. Ciszek, S.J., *He Leadeth Me* (Garden City, NY: Doubleday and Company, 1973), p. 143-148.

Chapter 15

1.   Rene Laurentin, pp. 96-97.

2.   For a deeper understanding of the phrase "deliver us from evil," we recommend the *Spiritual Warfare Prayer* by Dorothea Sudol, 108 Aberdeen St., Lowell, MA 01850 ($3.00 shipping included).

3.   Kevin Shanley, O. Carm., "A Moment's Peace," Aylesford, Darien, IL. Used with permission.

4.   Walter Ciszek, p. 143-148.

5.   Stefano Manelli, O.F.M., Conv., S.T.D., *Jesus our Eucharistic Love.* (Our Blessed Lady of Victory Mission, R.R. #2, Box 25, Brookings, SD, 1973), p. 125.

6.   *I am Your Jesus of Mercy,* p. 11.

Chapter 17

1.   Father Kenneth Roberts, "Loving People Back," *New Covenant,* Ann Arbor, MI, October 1989, p. 12.

2. Joanne Winchester, "Like the Swallows of Capistrano," Camp Lejeune, NC. Used with permission.

Appendix

1. For a study of this topic I recommend my book, *Intergenerational Healing*, which may be obtained from 108 Aberdeen Street, Lowell, MA 01850.

OTHER BOOKS OF INTEREST

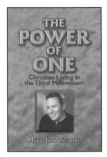

OTHER BOOKS OF INTEREST

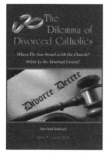

Additional Titles Published by Resurrection Press,
a Catholic Book Publishing Imprint

A Rachel Rosary *Larry Kupferman*	$4.50
Blessings All Around *Dolores Leckey*	$8.95
Catholic Is Wonderful *Mitch Finley*	$4.95
The Dilemma of Divorced Catholics *John Catoir*	$8.95
Discernment *Chris Aridas*	$8.95
Feasts of Life *Jim Vlaun*	$12.95
Grace Notes *Lorraine Murray*	$9.95
Healing through the Mass *Robert DeGrandis, SSJ*	$9.95
Healing Your Grief *Ruthann Williams, OP*	$7.95
Heart Peace *Adolfo Quezada*	$9.95
How Shall We Become Holy? *Mary Best*	$6.95
How Shall We Celebrate? *Lorraine Murray*	$6.95
How Shall We Pray? *James Gaffney*	$5.95
The Joy of Being an Altar Server *Joseph Champlin*	$5.95
The Joy of Being a Bereavement Minister *Nancy Stout*	$5.95
The Joy of Being a Catechist *Gloria Durka*	$4.95
The Joy of Being a Eucharistic Minister *Mitch Finley*	$5.95
The Joy of Being a Lector *Mitch Finley*	$5.95
The Joy of Being an Usher *Gretchen Hailer, RSHM*	$5.95
The Joy of Marriage Preparation *McDonough/Marinelli*	$5.95
The Joy of Music Ministry *J.M. Talbot*	$6.95
The Joy of Pilgrimage *Lori Erickson*	$6.95
The Joy of Praying the Psalms *Nancy de Flon*	$5.95
The Joy of Praying the Rosary *James McNamara*	$5.95
The Joy of Preaching *Rod Damico*	$6.95
The Joy of Teaching *Joanmarie Smith*	$5.95
The Joy of Worshiping Together *Rod Damico*	$5.95
Lessons for Living from the 23rd Psalm *Victor Parachin*	$6.95
Lights in the Darkness *Ave Clark, O.P.*	$8.95
Loving Yourself for God's Sake *Adolfo Quezada*	$5.95
Magnetized by God *Robert E. Lauder*	$8.95
Meditations for Survivors of Suicide *Joni Woelfel*	$8.95
Mercy Flows *Rod Damico*	$9.95
Mother Teresa *Eugene Palumbo, S.D.B.*	$5.95
Mourning Sickness *Keith Smith*	$8.95
Our Grounds for Hope *Fulton J. Sheen*	$7.95
Personally Speaking *Jim Lisante*	$8.95
Power of One *Jim Lisante*	$9.95
Praying the Lord's Prayer with Mary *Muto/vanKaam*	$8.95
5-Minute Miracles *Linda Schubert*	$4.95
Sabbath Moments *Adolfo Quezada*	$6.95
Season of New Beginnings *Mitch Finley*	$4.95
Sometimes I Haven't Got a Prayer *Mary Sherry*	$8.95
St. Katharine Drexel *Daniel McSheffery*	$12.95
What He Did for Love *Francis X. Gaeta*	$5.95
Woman Soul *Pat Duffy, OP*	$7.95
You Are My Beloved *Mitch Finley*	$10.95

For a free catalog call 1-800-892-6657
www.catholicbookpublishing.com